Sometimes I Forget

Sometimes I Forget

60 REMINDERS of HOPE for Your Hard Days

Julie Sunne

Copyright © 2024 by Julie Sunne
All rights reserved.
Printed in the United States of America

978-1-4300-8201-9

Published by B&H Publishing Group
Brentwood, Tennessee

Dewey Decimal Classification: 231
Subject Heading: GOD / GOD—PROMISES / PRAYER

Unless otherwise noted all Scripture is taken from the Christian Standard Bible. Copyright © 2017 by Holman Bible Publishers. Used by permission. Christian Standard Bible®, and CSB® are federally registered trademarks of Holman Bible Publishers, all rights reserved.

Scripture references marked ESV are taken from the English Standard Version. ESV® Text Edition: 2016. Copyright © 2001 by Crossway Bibles, a publishing ministry of Good News Publishers.

Scripture references marked NIV are taken from the New International Version®, NIV® Copyright ©1973, 1978, 1984, 2011 by Biblica, Inc.® Used by permission. All rights reserved worldwide.

Cover design by Jennifer Allison, Studio Nth.
Cover illustration by TWINS DESIGN STUDIO/Shutterstock.
Author photo by Lori Kartman.

1 2 3 4 5 6 • 27 26 25 24

To Hubby—the one who's weathered it all
with me and still has my heart

and

To Dan, Zach, Rach, and Joey—the ones
whose very lives remind me of hope

Acknowledgments

This book came together during a time of great stress and sorrow for me as I walked through the illness and death of both of my parents. I could not have completed it without the tremendous support and prayers of many and the sustaining grace of God. My most heartfelt thanks go out to all of you.

My husband, David: From insisting I spend as much time as needed with Mom and Dad, to giving me space to focus on this work, you provided in more ways than I can count. I am better because of you; the completion of this book is a testament to that. I love you forever.

My children, Daniel, Zachary, Rachel, and Joseph and Brooke: Life would be drab indeed without all of you in my life. You cheer me up and cheer me on, you are quick to offer help, and perhaps most importantly, you play games with me. You mean the world to me. I'm so grateful for your support during the writing of this book and for allowing me to include a little of your stories in its pages. I love you more than you'll ever know. A special thank you to Daniel for helping me brainstorm and edit (sometimes into the wee hours). You deserve extra peanut butter cups this year.

My publishing team at B&H Publishing, Ashley, Clarissa, and all the behind-the-scenes superstars: You do stellar work, and I couldn't ask for a more supportive and understanding group of individuals to work with. I am especially grateful for your grace during some of the most difficult days of my life.

My literary agent, Dan Balow with the Steve Laube Agency: You believed in me when I had little to attract an agent, helped me sift and hone my ideas, and championed this project. You gave me a chance, for which I will be forever grateful.

My theological text reviewer, Rev. Robert Snitzer: Your careful and critical review of the attributes I chose and my application of each one gave me the confidence to push "send." I am indebted.

My mom and dad, now in heaven: It's impossible to believe you're gone. You always encouraged me and were so excited for me when I landed this contract. How I wish you could see the end product. When you went to be with Jesus, you took a piece of my heart. Until we meet again . . .

My mother-in-law: Your faith inspires me. Your love blesses me.

My siblings, siblings-in-law, nieces, and nephews: I love my family. What a blessing to know you are always there for me.

My dearest friends and church family: Your support and prayers have been a source of great comfort and peace through the years. I am grateful for each of you. Special shout-outs to Wayne and Jan, Michael and Amie, and Rev. Dave and Darla, for so many reasons.

My readers and blog and social media followers: You honor me with your trust. May I prove worthy of it.

My Lord and Savior: Not only have You saved a wretch like me, but You help me produce fruit where a withered branch would otherwise exist. I can never fully understand You, but I can unequivocally trust You. Help me die more to self and live more for You. To You I offer all praise and glory!

Contents

Introduction	1
1. God Is Sovereign	3
2. God Is Incomparable	7
3. God Is Self-Sufficient	10
4. God Is Infinite	13
5. God Is Immutable	16
6. God Is Creative	19
7. God Is Righteous	22
8. God Is Loving	24
9. God Is Good	27
10. God Is Just	30
11. God Is Omnipotent	33
12. God Is Omnipresent	36
13. God Is Omniscient	39
14. God Is Kind	42
15. God Is Merciful	45
16. God Is Faithful	48
17. God Is Triune	50
18. God Is Simple	53
19. God Is Wise	56
20. God Is Holy	58

21. God Is Gracious	61
22. God Is Attentive	64
23. God Is Glorious	67
24. God Is Patient	70
25. God Is Impeccable	73
26. God Is Jealous	77
27. God Is Protective	80
28. God Is Transcendent	83
29. God Is Immanent	86
30. God Is Invisible	89
31. God Is Comforting	92
32. God Is Victorious	95
33. God Is Truthful	98
34. God Is Lifegiving	102
35. God Is Light	105
36. God Is Blessed	108
37. God Is Perfect	111
38. God Is Eternal	114
39. God Is Majestic	117
40. God Is Peaceful	120
41. God Is Steadfast	123
42. God Is Incomprehensible	126
43. God Is Impassible	129
44. God Is Forgiving	132

45. God Is Healing	135
46. God Is Spirit	138
47. God Is Sanctifying	141
48. God Is Wrathful	144
49. God Is Compassionate	147
50. God Is Immeasurable	150
51. God Is Sustaining	153
52. God Is Free	156
53. God Is Miraculous	159
54. God Is Joyful	162
55. God Is Approachable	165
56. God Is Generous	169
57. God Is Personal	172
58. God Is Foreknowing	174
59. God Is Shepherding	177
60. God Is Redemptive	180
Conclusion: Hope Is There in the Furnace of Affliction	183
Notes	187

Introduction

"It would be a good thing if young people were wise and old people were strong, but God has arranged things better."
MARTIN LUTHER[1]

I asked God to spare the life of my first baby. He did . . . by taking her home to be with Him. Not the ending I wanted, but perhaps the beginning I needed.

Right or Wrong, Good or Bad

Most of us are taught from an early age the concepts of right and wrong, good and bad. We're told to avoid bad and embrace what's right. And we're assured that God is good. However, the death of a baby doesn't fit in my definitions of either right or good. Neither does disability. So how can they fit into our understanding of a good and right God?

I didn't deem it good when my firstborn was born with a damaged arm. I didn't see anything good or right about my five miscarriages. It certainly didn't seem right for my daughter to be born with intellectual and physical disabilities. But somehow through the years, fruits of goodness and rightness grew from the roots of these occurrences. Somehow God transformed the worst situations in my life to ones filled with purpose and promise.

But how do we trust there's beauty when all we see is the ugly of a stage 4 cancer diagnosis? How do we find joy again after the death of a spouse? How do we trust God for good when a son or daughter disowns us? How do we walk in faith in the midst of disability? How do we hold onto hope when our world is falling apart? We get to know the One who gave us life.

Travel with me through the pages of this book as we learn more about this glorious, divine being we call Lord. On the way, we will explore sixty of His attributes. We will pray, surrender, and remember who our God is. We will find our faith strengthened and our hope renewed as we trust His promises anew.

> "'This is what the LORD says:
>
> The wise person should not boast in his wisdom;
> the strong should not boast in his strength;
> the wealthy should not boast in his wealth.
> But the one who boasts should boast in this:
> that he understands and knows me—
> that I am the LORD, showing faithful love,
> justice, and righteousness on the earth,
> for I delight in these things.
> This is the LORD's declaration.'"
> (Jer. 9:23–24)
>
> *"Encountering God changes everything."*
> SUSIE LARSON[2]

1: God Is Sovereign

Sometimes I forget, Lord, that You are *sovereign*, ruling over all and exercising Your perfect will. . . .

> God will bring this about in his own time. He is the blessed and only Sovereign, the King of kings, and the Lord of lords. (1 Tim. 6:15)

"The sovereignty of God is the one impregnable rock to which the suffering human heart must cling. The circumstances surrounding our lives are no accident; they may be the work of evil, but that evil is held firmly within the mighty hand of our sovereign God."

MARGARET CLARKSON[3]

"Dear Lord,

As I look at Rachel. Her well-formed body—outwardly complete, yet inwardly somehow different. I wonder, is this a mistake—a disability as we call it—something that went wrong? Or, somehow, is this how it should be? Is this exactly how You made her?

When her little cells were dividing, did You tell them to divide a little differently, or perhaps stay together instead of parting company?

Did You have plans so great for her that You had to create her as one of the least?

I know You weren't surprised, Lord, when she was born with a hole in the roof of her mouth, heart anomalies, and an inability to keep acid from scorching her throat.

Sometimes I Forget

I know You didn't look down shocked from Your lofty perch and whisper to Your angels, 'Something went wrong; this little girl is going to develop slower than most children.'

No, Father, You knew all along. You always know.

You knit her together in the womb just as You do every other being on earth (Ps. 139:13). In fact, before the foundation of the world, You knew her and already planned for her salvation (Eph. 1:3–5).

I know these things, Lord. But . . .

Sometimes it is so hard. Sometimes this world blinds me to the possibilities that exist in Your magnificent realm. Sometimes I forget that with only a word, You spoke the entire universe into existence. That You breathed, and man walked and talked.

Sometimes I forget that You are the Director of the sun and moon. That the winds and rain answer only to You. That, with a wave of Your hand, the mountains move.

It's just that some days are so difficult in my humanness, Father. Life gets chaotic and hard, and amnesia wipes hope from this finite mind of mine."

I ended this prayer of lament and hope about my daughter that I published in a blog post more than a decade ago with these words: "Hope may disappear from view for a time, but the closer I draw to You, the less I need to see Hope to know it's there. Because You are Hope, Lord, and You never leave us."

As a young mother, I'm not sure my prayer would have ended so hope-filled, but I have learned something about God's nature as I've grown in faith: He is always working in my life as a loving Father. I don't always like what He allows in my life. Often, I don't see the purpose or the goodness. But I know He vets everything He allows, so I can accept it as His perfect and holy will. God exercises His sovereignty not based on what makes us comfortable, but on what will edify and refine us. The account of Job gives us a clear picture of His sovereignty in action.

Sometimes I Forget

The Lord gave permission to Satan to afflict Job with many hardships (Job 1:6–12). From the death of all of his children, the destruction of his livestock, and the presence of painful boils covering his body, Job greatly suffered and didn't know why. It seemed cruel. However, later, God allows us a glimpse of His redemptive purpose in the torment as Job obediently intercedes for his friends. God, in His sovereignty, allowed horrible suffering to achieve His plan. Job didn't suffer for naught. And whether we can see it or not, our suffering is never for nothing. God's hand is in it all.

So, no, God did not make a mistake when He created Rachel. He never makes mistakes. Like the blind man in John 9:3, she is a beautiful part of His plan to bless and transform, "so that God's works might be displayed."

Whatever difficult situation we face, the God of the universe is in charge of it. Whether large issues or seemingly small ones, He knows what's going on, and He has a plan. As the Sovereign, He is allowing the hardship in this season for a reason. We may not understand, but when we accept the mystery of the Divine Supreme Being, believing He has control over all and is never caught off guard, we can choose trust over worry. We can look into our unexpected situation with expectancy for how He will use it in our lives—remembering He's guiding it all.

Sometimes I forget, Lord, that You are sovereign, *ruling over all and exercising Your perfect will, that You have divine control over everything that happens. I forget that everything I face has been approved by You for a holy and right purpose. My finite mind cannot always understand. Often, I only sense hardship. Comfort me, Lord, in my confusion and pain. Remind me that what looks chaotic and even scary to me is not leaving You wringing Your hands. You are allowing me to experience this season for a reason.*

Sometimes I Forget

Help me look with expectancy for how You will use it in my life. And help me trust You when You take me down a path different from the one I would choose.

TRUTH REMINDER
Nothing comes to me that doesn't
first go through the Lord, and all He allows
and determines has a good and right purpose.

2: God Is Incomparable

Sometimes I forget, Lord, that You are *incomparable*, unequaled and matchless in all ways. . . .

> With whom will you compare God? What likeness will you set up for comparison with him? . . . "To whom will you compare me, or who is my equal?" asks the Holy One. (Isa. 40:18, 25)

"Everything about God is great, vast, incomparable. He never forgets, never fails, never falters, never forfeits His word. To every declaration of promise or prophecy the Lord has exactly adhered, every engagement of covenant or threatening He will make good."
ARTHUR W. PINK[4]

The storm had been threatening for the last few hours. Finally, the sky released its fury. The rain and wind pummeled us, but it was the lightning that chased us off the lake. We paddled hard to get to shore.

My husband took charge of securing our canoes while I sought shelter from the storm for us and our three boys. It wasn't much, but the low-hanging branches of a pine tree afforded protection from the worst of the rain. We took what we could get. Thankfully, we don't need to settle when it comes to our Lord.

Few of us enjoy being tossed around in a storm: whether a literal one or a figurative disturbance in our lives. We'd prefer to be sheltered from the effects of either kind. Unfortunately, we don't always look in the right place when (not if) the storms of life hit. We trust in our own strength to anchor us until the squall passes. Sometimes we turn to others for help. Occasionally, we even ignore the need for refuge.

Each of these can sometimes be effective. However, when our hearts are fearful and hurting, we need an anchor that will never fail us, a shelter that is infinitely strong and always present. That security can only be found "in the shadow of the Almighty" (Ps. 91:1), the supreme Lord, the sovereign and all-powerful One.

The Most High offers unshakable and unchanging promises. Promises to provide what we need to weather any storm. He'll set us high upon a rock (Ps. 27:5). He'll hide us under His wings (Ps. 91:4). He'll shield and protect us. And one day He'll wipe away all our tears (Isa. 25:8; Rev. 21:4). In His supremacy, He is incomparable. Who else can speak the universe into existence? What other being can control the winds and rain? Where else can we find one who will never falter, never forget, and never fail us? And who else would give up their life for the forgiveness of our sins?

Nothing can equal the Lord's strength, wisdom, peace, mercy, love, and holiness. Nothing can be as compassionate, generous, gracious, majestic, perfect, comforting, and knowledgeable. No one can compare to the Creator of the universe. He is unmatched in character and in action.

King David realized this truth, but he also knew how easy it is to forget. So he wrote about the hope he found in the Almighty. He sang about the greatness of God. He penned poems and prayers acknowledging the Rock that would never fail him. He reminded himself of the promises found in the Lord by praising Him.

Like David, we also struggle with remembering where our true security lies. Life distracts. Our pride rears its ugly head. Other options entice. So let's offer ourselves reminders of where to look, like this praise the king tucked into a psalm of thanksgiving and cry for help:

Sometimes I Forget

> Lord my God, you have done many things—
> your wondrous works and your plans for us;
> none can compare with you.
> If I were to report and speak of them,
> they are more than can be told. (Ps. 40:5)

Scripture assures us that nothing and no one is mightier or more trustworthy than our Lord. So why would we place our security anywhere else? With the help of the Holy Spirit, let's begin to live with our faith firmly planted in the Incomparable.

Sometimes I forget, Lord, that You are incomparable, *unequaled and matchless in all ways. I forget that no one can replace Your faithfulness, love, and power. No one can be more righteous or compassionate. Nothing else could defeat death itself and provide for my salvation. Remind me, Lord, of Your perfect nature, the standard by which every other being is measured and falls short. Help me plant my faith firmly in You, trusting You and You alone for my security.*

TRUTH REMINDER
Only the Lord can provide the security I long
for, security that will last for eternity.

3: God Is Self-Sufficient

Sometimes I forget, Lord, that You are *self-sufficient*, existing independent of anyone or anything. . . .

> The God who made the world and everything in it—he is Lord of heaven and earth—does not live in shrines made by hands. Neither is he served by human hands, as though he needed anything, since he himself gives everyone life and breath and all things. (Acts 17:24–25)

> *"Fountain of good, all blessing flows*
> *From Thee; no want Thy fullness knows;*
> *What but Thyself canst Thou desire?*
> *Yet, self-sufficient as Thou art,*
> *Thou dost desire my worthless heart.*
> *This, only this, dost Thou require."*
>
> JOHANN SCHEFFLER[5]

Before my feet hit the floor in the morning, my mind is running to complete my to-do list. Bible reading, prayer, ministry work, editing, gardening, food prep, housecleaning, laundry—I strive to make it all happen. No boredom here; there's too much to do, and I think it's all up to me.

But is it really? Who told me that? If I'm honest, my pride. I don't want to look weak. I don't want to let my people down. I don't want to be seen as incompetent, undependable, or unworthy. Yet I run myself ragged chasing after everything without

Sometimes I Forget

seeking God's thing(s). I lose my joy as I seek the world's accolades instead of God's anointing. I miss out on the blessing of *being* as I bow to a doctrine of *doing*.

Many of us fall into the trap of thinking we are indispensable. It cripples our service to others and our worship of, and relationship to, the Lord. We err in believing God needs us to do our part for His plan to be enacted. Although such thinking is well intended, it falls short of the truth. God *can* use us (and will, if we have a willing spirit), but He doesn't *need* us.

God is the only One who is needed, the only One truly self-sufficient. He doesn't need anyone or anything. Our service, our tithe, our obedience serves a purpose for us, not Him. It's true, the Lord does have a plan. He does have a place for us in fulfilling that plan. But it's important for us to remember that although God delights in us, His children, His plan is not dependent on us.

It's beautiful, really! A critical characteristic we often overlook, God's self-sufficiency, means we can breathe a bit easier. It's not up to us; His plan will be fulfilled no matter how well we perform. And because He doesn't depend on anything or anyone else, He never runs out of grace, mercy, kindness, power, wisdom, peace. . . . His well never runs dry. His abundance flows endlessly. Therefore, when we do step out to serve Him in obedience and love, not out of some skewed sense of "have to," we don't have to worry we won't be enough or won't have enough to do the tasks laid before us. God has all He needs, so He will be the *enough* for us.

Sometimes I forget, Lord, that You are self-sufficient, *existing independent of anyone or anything, that You need no one, that You have all You need in Yourself. I forget that You can satisfy all our needs because Your well of goodness, peace, mercy, and grace never*

Sometimes I Forget

dries up. Help me remember that You don't need my help to fulfill Your plan, although You do have a place in that plan for me if I choose to step into it. You delight in me, Lord, not in what I can or cannot do. You are perfectly capable without me, but I desperately need You. Help me remember Your sufficiency for when I do serve in love and obedience.

TRUTH REMINDER
God delights in me,
not in what I can or cannot do.

4: God Is Infinite

Sometimes I forget, Lord, that You are *infinite*, unlimited in all ways. . . .

> "I am the Alpha and the Omega," says the Lord God, "the one who is, who was, and who is to come, the Almighty." (Rev. 1:8)

"An infinite God can give all of Himself to each of His children. He does not distribute Himself that each may have a part, but to each one He gives all of Himself as fully as if there were no others."

A. W. TOZER[6]

Fear and anxiety gripped me. I struggled to squeeze out words between the sobs, to impart lucid thoughts to my oldest son two hundred miles away. In the span of thirty minutes, I went from competent to desperate. Nothing had changed, but suddenly I was hit full force by the enormity of an unknown future for my daughter. Panic about Rachel's future had never seized me so powerfully. The thought of dying doesn't wreck me, but the idea of leaving my daughter behind does.

As a functionally nonverbal young adult with the intellectual capability of a three-year-old, Rachel will always be at the mercy of whoever cares for her. That raises many concerns for when my husband and I are no longer here. Will her future caregivers protect her? Will they provide appropriate care, keeping her clean and well fed? What about her emotional and spiritual needs? Will they address those? Will they ensure she keeps warm while

Sometimes I Forget

sleeping and that she has her favorite stuffed animal or pink blanket? If not, how can she let her needs be known?

I longed for answers that would calm my mother's heart. But despite their best intentions, neither my son nor the few friends to whom I sent a panicked text could provide them. No one can. This world holds pain and brokenness for each of us, and we're limited in how much we can control.

On that awful day, I needed to believe in something beyond my understanding, something bigger than human capability. I needed to believe that Rachel would never be left alone. I needed assurance for her future.

And that can only come from the One who transcends time and space, the Alpha and Omega. God, in His infinity, always was, always is, and always will be. No future stretches too far from Him. He's in the future before it begins. There's never too many of us and not enough of Him. He's never stretched too thin. The Lord's infinite nature means He knows no bounds and will be where we need Him when we need Him. And that includes being with my daughter when I no longer can.

Sometimes I forget, Lord, that You are infinite, *unlimited in all ways. You are the Alpha and the Omega; time and space do not hold You. I forget that You exist by Your own power, so that even when my situation seems impossible, it is possible for You. Remind me that, in Your infinity, You are never pulled in too many directions or stretched too thin. You do not run out of time. Help me remember, Lord, that no matter how great the ask, as a personal God with no beginning and no end, You will be where I need You, when I need You.*

Sometimes I Forget

TRUTH REMINDER
No matter how scary the future looks,
God will always be where
I need Him when I need Him.

5: God Is Immutable

Sometimes I forget, Lord, that You are *immutable*, unchanging for all eternity. . . .

> Jesus Christ is the same yesterday, today, and forever. (Heb. 13:8)

"There is unwavering peace today when an uncertain tomorrow is trusted to an unchanging God."
ANN VOSKAMP[7]

With an exhausted wave of her hand, Mom bid me call the Veteran's Affairs Medical Clinic. It was time. We had no choice. Mom needed help to keep Dad home and herself healthy. His frailty, confusion, and memory loss had reached the point where Mom could no longer care for him without help. Looking from one parent to the other, my heart broke seeing the emotions play across their faces: Dad, forlorn and lost; Mom, resigned and sad.

Dialing the number, I begged God for comfort and strength. No one could tell us how long Dad's decline would continue before the Lord took Him home. All I could do then—all any of us can do in situations like that—is lean on God, trusting in His sovereignty, love, and faithfulness. I breathed a prayer for Mom and Dad, that they, too, would draw comfort and strength from Him.

Somewhere along the way, it seems many of us develop the wrong idea of what our life should look like, especially as we age. After many long years of working and raising a family, we expect to relax in our latter years. However, those golden years are often fraught with health and financial issues. Aches and pains settle in to stay. Our walk turns into a shuffle. The independence we cherish gives way to needing help with previously easy things like walking and getting dressed, draining our pride and our bank accounts.

Whether our difficulties stem from age or other circumstances, we all eventually face undesirable circumstances. In our struggle, it can be hard to remember that the God we depended on in our healthier and easier years remains the God we can depend on in our more difficult seasons. He has not changed.

I've struggled seeing my once vibrant, strong, independent Dad reduced to a shell of who he was. I've wondered about the purpose God has in leaving Dad on earth in a state he fears and hates. I'm concerned about its effect on Mom. Still, I know the Lord remains the same loving, good, and faithful God I've always known. And He is carrying out His perfect and holy will.

Yes, our circumstances will change, our friendships will change, our bodies will change, but our Lord never will. He is still in control. We can still depend on Him to see us through. Regardless of what you see when you look at your life—the unexpected, the hard, the sad—be assured that it is not a mistake, that God will be with you through it, and that He still loves you with an everlasting love. The very nature of God promises us that. His immutability gives us security in all His other attributes. God will never change, so we never need despair.

Sometimes I forget, Lord, that You are immutable, *unchanging for all eternity. I forget that Your nature does not shift with the winds. You don't feel and act a certain way one day, only to feel and act differently the next. Remind me that I can count on You to be as You always are–loving, just, holy, compassionate, forgiving– and that in Your immutability, I can trust all Your promises and believe all I read in the Scriptures. I don't fully comprehend why You allow the suffering You do, Lord, but help me remember that I can always trust You because You are the same yesterday, today, and forever!*

TRUTH REMINDER
God's promises to me and His love for me never change because He remains the same yesterday, today, and for all tomorrows.

6: God Is Creative

Sometimes I forget, Lord, that You are *creative*, purposely and wondrously making all that exists. . . .

> God saw all that he had made, and it was very good indeed. Evening came and then morning: the sixth day. (Gen. 1:31)

"You weren't an accident. You weren't mass produced. You aren't an assembly-line product. You were deliberately planned, specifically gifted, and lovingly positioned on the Earth by the Master Craftsman."
MAX LUCADO[8]

Although she assured me she liked it in the home in which she now resided, I could see it. I saw it in the way tears welled up as we visited. I saw it in her faraway look as she talked about the past. This dear old friend grieved the passing of the years. She missed the house she called home for so long. She missed attending church. She missed hanging with family and friends. She missed her independence.

During the decades that defined her life, my friend's time and talents were appreciated. Others needed her. They needed what she had to offer. Now, she rarely leaves her building and only sees those who seek her out. Her purpose is less evident, but no less prevalent.

When health issues, age, or some other circumstance prevent us from being active and helpful, we can feel lost and worthless.

Thankfully, what we do and are capable of doing doesn't define our worth; God does. And humans have immense worth because we are made in God's image.

God, as Creator, made the heavens and earth and all that dwell in them. Then He went a step further and created a being to rule over the other created beings. And He chose to make this creation in His image! Yes, you and I are made in the image of God, and as God's image-bearers, we resemble Him in spirit. This means we reflect His character as we engage and interact in life. So, when we make a good choice, we reflect His holiness. When we reason, we reflect His intellect. When we socialize, we reflect His triune nature and love.

Of course, this reflection is imperfect, marred by sin. Nonetheless, what we say and do has profound purpose in reflecting the Lord to others. Even if all we can do is smile, that smile demonstrates God's love and kindness.

I've seen how damaging feeling purposeless can be. If left unchecked, it creates doubt as to our very worth. But we have evidence of our immense value: We have the ability to think and plan, choose freely, and fellowship with others. These very traits scream worth as an *imago dei*, a valued being, created to reflect the Creator. As a potter forms a vessel for his use, so God formed man for His purpose. Therefore, when circumstances blind us to our worth, we need to remind ourselves that, as God's image-bearers, formed with His loving hands for His use, we have purpose as long as we have breath.

Sometimes I forget, Lord, that You are creative, *purposely and wondrously making all that exists, including me. And sometimes I forget that You chose to create man in Your image to give You glory as we reflect You mentally, morally, and socially. And although sin has marred the image, every time I reason, make a*

Sometimes I Forget

good choice, or engage in fellowship, I still reflect You, however imperfect the reflection. But sometimes, Lord, I feel worthless and rudderless. Please remind me that You set me apart, creating me on purpose for a purpose. Help me remember that, as Your child, I have immense worth, that my life on earth has great value. And remind me that the purpose You've endowed me with remains until I breathe my last.

TRUTH REMINDER
God created me in His image, giving me purpose as long as I have breath.

7: God Is Righteous

Sometimes I forget, Lord, that You are *righteous*, virtuous in all You do. . . .

> The LORD is righteous in all his ways
> and faithful in all his acts. (Ps. 145:17)

"Our righteousness is in Him, and our hope depends, not upon the exercise of grace in us, but upon the fullness of grace and love in Him, and upon His obedience unto death."
JOHN NEWTON[9]

Tears greeted me as I entered my son's room to tuck him in for the night. I knelt next to his bed to learn the cause. Between sobs, he managed to communicate his pain. He had made a terrible choice, one that made my heart hurt too. And he was scared. Would God still love him? Would he be rejected by his heavenly Father for his sin?

Oh, Son! There is grace for all our sins. I wrapped him tight and whispered this truth to both of us. God loves His children, and He wants none to be lost. He made a way where there was no way. It's true, God demands righteousness, but it's also true that, through the sacrifice of the Lord Jesus Christ, He imputed His righteousness to us. We can't make it on our own. But thank God, we don't have to.

Satan loves to accuse us of our sin, of how we've fallen short, of how we'll never measure up to God's standards. I suppose he's right. This side of heaven, we won't ever be good enough, generous enough, holy enough. We'll always fail our children, fail our spouses, fail our God. But we're not left there. God doesn't label us "failure." And He doesn't assign us to sit forever in the back row either. Our poor choices don't make us failures. They make us sinners in need of a Savior. They diagnose a sickness that needs the ultimate Healer. They put us in a place to receive His fullness, so we can then pour it out to others.

The enemy would have us believe our inability to walk righteously on our own makes us worthless. The truth is God calls the sickest and most infirm to Him. He pours His worth into our worthlessness. He graciously offers us sinners His righteousness. No longer relegated to the back row, God welcomes us to the front to drink deeply from His well. And it's when we finally acknowledge the desperation of our condition that we find healing. That is when we can receive the Great Physician's best medicine as we move to wholeness in Him.

> *Sometimes I forget, Lord, that You are* righteous, *virtuous in all You do. I forget that, thanks to the work of Jesus Christ on the cross, You have redeemed me. Believing I'll never measure up, I let Satan beat me down. Remind me, dear Lord, that while it's true I can never achieve righteousness on my own, I don't have to. You freed me from that burden. Help me remember that You are infinitely, unchangingly perfect and holy and that You graciously cover me with Your righteousness. I am worthy in Christ. Thank You for making a way where there was no way.*

TRUTH REMINDER
God covers me with His righteousness, assuring my place in heaven even when I stumble in my walk of faith.

8: God Is Loving

Sometimes I forget, Lord, that You are *loving*, having deep affection for all equally and unfailingly. . . .

> The one who does not love does not know God, because God is love. God's love was revealed among us in this way: God sent his one and only Son into the world so that we might live through him. Love consists in this: not that we loved God, but that he loved us and sent his Son to be the atoning sacrifice for our sins. (1 John 4:8–10)

"God's unfailing love for us is an objective fact affirmed over and over in the Scriptures. It is true whether we believe it or not. Our doubts do not destroy God's love, nor does our faith create it. It originates in the very nature of God, who is love, and it flows to us through our union with His beloved Son."

JERRY BRIDGES[10]

I've never heard my twenty-five-year-old daughter say, "I love you." Not with her own voice. She can't. Severe speech apraxia combined with intellectual disability prevents that exchange. It'd be delightful to hear those words from her. However, I never doubt her love for me because not a day goes by that she does not express it in a tangible, meaningful way.

We all want to hear those three little words. We all want to know we're loved. To feel cherished and valued deep within. It's such a powerful desire, we often go to unhealthy extremes to

Sometimes I Forget

fulfill it. We try to earn it. We give into the wishes of others to secure their affection. We do all we can to be on the receiving end of love.

But live long in this world and you'll know the pain of feeling unloved. Someone at some time will let us down. They'll reject our love and withhold their own. But there's One whose love never ends. God's unconditional love, His *agape* love, stands steadfast for all eternity.

Still, sometimes circumstances make us doubt His love. He doesn't audibly voice it, so pain can easily blind us to it. Yet God's love is not fickle nor conditional. He perfectly loves us for eternity. His love is not dependent on what we do or don't do, and it won't ever run out or be spread too thin. No, the Lord doesn't directly verbalize His love for us, but like my daughter, He does make it known in a variety of ways. In His Holy Word, in the beauty found in nature, in the mercy He daily extends to us, in friendships and new life, and ultimately in the incarnation and sacrifice of His Son Jesus Christ, the Lord demonstrates His everlasting love each and every day. As our Father, He gives agape love to us freely and completely, so we never need to feel unloved.

> *Sometimes I forget, Lord, that You are loving, having deep affection for all equally and unfailingly. I sometimes forget that You love me perfectly and completely–forever. My circumstances often make me wonder if it's true, looking anything but loving. Remind me, Lord, that loving is not merely something You do; it is a part of Your being, and nothing can separate Your love from me. It is agape, unconditional. Remind me, Lord, that You value me so highly that You sent Your only Son to die for me, and nothing I do or don't do will change that truth or Your affection for me. Help me love others with the love You have for me.*

Sometimes I Forget

TRUTH REMINDER
God loves me with an everlasting love,
confirmed not by my circumstances but by
the sacrifice of Jesus on the cross.

9: God Is Good

Sometimes I forget, Lord, that You are *good*, infinitely right, true, and noble. . . .

> I am certain that I will see the Lord's goodness
> in the land of the living. (Ps. 27:13)

"This is true faith, a living confidence in the goodness of God."
MARTIN LUTHER[11]

"Help me! Girls, help me get out!" The elderly lady implored us with her outstretched hand, her pleading eyes narrowed in desperation. My sister and I had stumbled into the memory care unit of the apartment community where our parents had recently moved. We hadn't meant to go there, but in our exploration of the facility, we opened a door to a scene that haunted me for months. The wheelchair-bound lady followed us, propelling herself with one good leg, begging to be rescued.

We tried to assure her. Hush her, maybe. Sweat trickled down my back. I glanced at my sister; she seemed equally agitated. I mouthed to her, "Sorry," as we glanced around, waiting to be let out of the ward.

Hurry, let us out! I silently urged the nurses' aides. It couldn't have lasted five minutes, but it seemed like an eternity. As we stepped into the freedom this dear lady longed for, I tried to shake off the weight of sadness that had settled on me. But it followed me as tenaciously as she had. How unfair for this poor soul to languish in between the now and eternity. Why didn't God end her suffering by taking her home?

It's an age-old question: If God is good, why does He allow suffering? Why does He allow the elderly and infirm to languish in pain and confusion? Why does He allow children to suffer unimaginable horrors at the hands of those they should be able to trust? Why are some kind and caring women barren while other selfish, neglectful women have many babies? Why do some die so young? Why is there Christian persecution? I'm afraid I don't have a pat answer. But I do know that God is good and will only be good. What He allows or orchestrates cannot be or lead to anything but what is right, true, and noble. And since the Lord is unchanging, we know His goodness will always be.

The Lord and His goodness reach far beyond our comprehension. He is omniscient and wise. His goodness is pure and infinite. As finite beings, we cannot begin to know what He knows or understand what He understands. (And if we could, would He be worthy of our worship?) But we can trust His character. As a perfect and loving God, we know that He will be with us in our suffering and will bring something good out of it. And in that lies a sure and certain hope.

> *Sometimes I forget, Lord, that You are good, infinitely right, true, and noble. I forget that all You allow will be good or be used for our ultimate good. I struggle to make sense of broken and ugly circumstances. I wonder why You would allow such difficult things in the lives of those You love. Remind me, Lord, that good is defined in Your very being. Nothing but what is right and true can come from You. Help me remember that nothing is impossible for You, so what looks dark and wrong will be made right in the end. Strengthen my faith to trust You when what I see doesn't support who I know You to be.*

Sometimes I Forget

TRUTH REMINDER
God remains good even when my situation is not, and He will bring good out of it.

10: God Is Just

Sometimes I forget, Lord, that You are *just*, morally upright in all Your dealings. . . .

> The works of his [the Lord's] hands are truth
> and justice;
> all his instructions are trustworthy.
> They are established forever and ever,
> enacted in truth and in uprightness.
> (Ps. 111:7–8)

"The justice of God is always and ever an expression of His holy character. . . . What God does is always consistent with who God is."

R. C. SPROUL[12]

My toddler son's blue eyes pleaded with me. "Don't let them hurt me, Mommy!" Desperation laced his little voice. Chubby arms clamped around my neck. I tried to soothe him. To help him understand the importance of getting this shot. But nothing I said helped. All his two-year-old mind could focus on was how much it would hurt. He couldn't comprehend that this painful thing was actually good for him—that my love demanded I allow him to be hurt for his own good.

I get it, because I too often feel the same way about the painful things in my life. They don't make sense. All I can focus on is how much it hurts. My finite "toddler" mind can't comprehend that suffering could actually be good for me in the end. In my limited understanding, I struggle to see how allowing pain might actually be loving and just. I think most of us do.

God allows situations that don't make sense to us; they seem cruel and unjust. A brother accidentally running over his sister. A single mom caring alone for her preteen son who has autism and out-of-control behavior. A teenager living as a quadriplegic after a diving accident. A husband and father slowly slipping into the depths of dementia. A young mother waking up to find her husband dead beside her. A young father being diagnosed with stomach cancer that brings horrific pain and an early death. An abusive mother becoming pregnant again, while a barren woman is left to agonize over her empty arms. In our minds these are all horrific circumstances. None seem just or right. Yet God in His infinite knowledge, wisdom, and sovereignty allowed them.

Why didn't He intervene? He could have. Wouldn't that be the just thing to do? It certainly seems like it to us. But God doesn't simply dabble in justice. He *is* just! We can trust that all He allows conforms to His just nature.

Difficult to understand? Impossible, really. That's why knowing God's character is so important to our faith walk. We cannot possibly comprehend the ways of an eternal, all-powerful, infinite God. But we can lean into His perfect, just, and unchanging nature and find rest there. We can take comfort in the fact that justice will be served, whether now on earth or in God's ultimate judgment in heaven. We can give thanks that the judgment we deserve was poured out on Jesus Christ on the cross; thus, justice is satisfied for all Christians.

Justice runs through all God allows. He never is more or less just, but always perfectly just. Even when we don't understand, we can take comfort in that truth. And one day, at the final judgment, all the injustices of the world will be made right.

Sometimes I Forget

Sometimes I forget, Lord, that You are just, morally upright in all Your dealings. I forget that You always make sound judgments steeped in love, mercy, and truth. I look at my circumstances and wonder where You are in all of this suffering and injustice. Forgive me for questioning You, Lord. After all, You gave up Your Son to take the penalty for my sins. Remind me that, although I may not understand, You always act in accord with Your righteous, merciful, and holy nature. Remind me that the burdens of this world are fleeting, and my suffering is temporary. Help me find rest in knowing that You will make right all of the injustices of this world at the final judgment.

TRUTH REMINDER

God is always perfectly just in what He allows in my life, and at the final judgment He will make right the injustices of this world.

11: God Is Omnipotent

Sometimes I forget, Lord, that You are *omnipotent*, all-powerful and always capable. . . .

> "Oh, LORD God! You yourself made the heavens and earth by your great power and with your outstretched arm. Nothing is too difficult for you!" (Jer. 32:17)
>
> *"God's power is like Himself: infinite, eternal, incomprehensible; it can neither be checked, restrained, nor frustrated by the creature."*
> STEPHEN CHARNOCK[13]

My hand in hers, I bent over Rachel's bed, resting my head on a pillow. I slumbered fitfully, waking often to nurses entering the room or my daughter's whimper as she stirred, confused and in pain.

For three days I stayed by Rachel's bedside, leaving only when someone insisted I take a break. It looked like I was muscling through my daughter's recovery. Years ago, that would have been the case, but no longer. Rach and I weren't the only two in that room during those long nights of her hospital stay. I had invited another. One who could and would carry us through—the Almighty.

An independently strong young woman, I felt certain I could handle all that the world threw at me—invincible and capable. Yet not too many years into married life, I began to have doubts. Trials piled up. Multiple miscarriages, the unending demands of

Sometimes I Forget

raising a child with disabilities, and countless other hardships revealed I wasn't as strong as I thought.

Being a strong woman isn't all bad. The problem lies in believing we can do it all on our own. One day, in some circumstance, our strength will fail us. We need a confidence in something more secure, something that will withstand any hardship. We need an assurance of a strength that never wanes. We need a hope beyond human reasoning. That hope and strength are only found in the Lord Almighty.

Not only is God all-knowing, all-caring, and ever faithful, He possesses unsurpassed power. With only a word He created a vast universe and all that resides in it. "He spread the land on the waters" (Ps. 136:6), "made the great lights" (v. 7), and supplies "food to every creature" (v. 25). Through miracles like parting the Red Sea (v. 13), providing manna (Exod. 16:4), and toppling the walls of Jericho (Josh. 6), He brought His people to the promised land of Canaan. Nothing is too hard for Him. He can overcome any obstacle. A confidence placed in the incomparable power of the Lord instead of the flimsy hope of the flesh will never disappoint.

> *Sometimes I forget, Lord, that You are* omnipotent, *all-powerful and always capable. I forget that, as the Almighty, none of Your plans can be thwarted and that You never fail. Lord, when I try to carry the load of my troubles alone, remind me that nothing short of divine will last. It's all futile and fragile. Remind me that whatever I place my hope in apart from You will fail me, including my flesh and the promises of this world. Help me remember, Lord, that only You have the power and strength to give me lasting hope. Help me surrender all my perceived strength and rest in Yours. Fill me with courage as I face the challenges ahead.*

Sometimes I Forget

TRUTH REMINDER
The Lord is powerful enough
to get me through any trial.

12: God Is Omnipresent

Sometimes I forget, Lord, that You are *omnipresent*, always everywhere. . . .

> "Am I a God who is only near"—this is the LORD's declaration—"and not a God who is far away? Can a person hide in secret places where I cannot see him?"—the LORD's declaration. "Do I not fill the heavens and the earth?"—the LORD's declaration. (Jer. 23:23–24)

"In my efforts to flee God, I will always end up some place where's He's at because I've never left where He was."
CRAIG D. LOUNSBROUGH[14]

Into the deepening shadows of the night I ran. Breath coming in gulps. A torrent of tears stinging my flushed face.

Exhausted, I finally sank to the dank ground, my scream piercing the wooded silence. The sound shot out from deep within—a desperate plea to release the pent-up pain threatening to overwhelm me once again. Another lost pregnancy, another baby gone before I could hold her. I felt alone, confused, and angry.

The Lord has promised to never "leave" me nor "forsake" me (Deut. 31:6; Heb. 13:5 NIV), yet circumstances had left me feeling isolated and abandoned that night—and in many other instances throughout my life. Through the years I've grappled with God's promises and my reality.

Sometimes I Forget

I struggled to believe His promises because they didn't match the expectations I had for how those promises should manifest in my life. I needed to know the One who promised He would deliver. I needed assurance He is faithful. Because promises are only as reliable as the one who is making them.

Looking back, I'm certain He was there then and has been with me during every affliction. I know because it's in His very nature to be so. In His omnipresence, He is everywhere present always, never turning His head. He is not bound to human constraints of time and space. He's not with me more now and with my neighbor more later. He has promised to be with each of us "always, to the end of the age" (Matt. 28:20).

God was with me that heart-wrenching night. He whispered His promises to pain-dampened ears, but He was there. I know because His goodness, mercy, and grace ministered to me in the weeks, months, and years after. As omnipresent, the Lord is always near. We can't run far enough to leave His presence. We can't go deep enough or high enough to escape His reach. No matter how minuscule the particle or vast the galaxy, God is fully present with it. How much more can we be assured He'll be present with His children? Some find that disconcerting, but when You consider the character of God in totality, His complete nature, it is a crowning grace to have the Lord of the universe always present.

Although my pain masked His presence that dark, damp night, *Jehovah Shammah* ("Jehovah is there") met me. He ministered to me in ways that continue to bear fruit. He'll meet you in your hard situation as well. Never doubt His presence, even when your pain blinds you to it. And take comfort in the truth that He'll never leave you alone.

Sometimes I Forget

Sometimes I forget, Lord, that You are omnipresent, always everywhere. You circumscribe the smallest particle and the largest galaxy. Sometimes I forget that Your very nature guarantees You are with me, You never turn Your head from me. I may not see You or sense Your presence, but I can trust I'm not alone. Still at times I feel forgotten and abandoned. Remind me, Lord, that You are with me even when I don't see You. When I call to You, reveal Yourself to me. In my trials, help me sense Your nearness. And help me take comfort in the truth that You'll never leave me alone.

TRUTH REMINDER
I am never alone; even when God doesn't reveal Himself, He is still present with me.

13: God Is Omniscient

Sometimes I forget, Lord, that You are *omniscient*, You know all. . . .

> Lord, you have searched me and known me.
> You know when I sit down and when I stand up;
> you understand my thoughts from far away.
> You observe my travels and my rest;
> you are aware of all my ways.
> Before a word is on my tongue,
> you know all about it, Lord. (Ps. 139:1–4)

"He is omniscient, which means that He knows in one free and effortless act all matter, all spirit, all relationships, all events."
A. W. TOZER[15]

Sweet lips clamped firmly shut. Arms warding me off. Eyes shredding this mama's heart. Her eyes, my daughter's big, beautiful brown eyes, always so full of love and mischief, were now reflecting hurt and confusion. Pleading with me to take away the pain. Not understanding why I had to force her to swallow that yucky stuff I called medicine.

It meant little to explain it would help her feel better; that didn't "make" it better now. Now she only knew I was instilling more discomfort. Tears trickling down my face and mumbling the old adage "this hurts me more than it hurts you," I held her flailing arms tight and squeezed the offending liquid into her mouth—doing my best to avoid those haunting eyes.

Sometimes I Forget

Releasing my daughter and wiping my tears, I whispered, "I'm sorry." And then I experienced a grace beyond measure: leaning forward, Rachel planted a breath of a kiss on my tear-stained cheek. A kiss of a thousand words. A kiss not just of forgiveness, but of her love and trust in me. A proclamation that although she didn't understand, she was willing to lean on my understanding.

It made me ponder how I respond to painful, frustrating, and confusing times and situations in my life. Rachel realized I knew more than she did about the situation and that I loved her. She trusted I wouldn't unnecessarily hurt her. Do I believe the same about God? That He knows more than I do? That He would never cause me unnecessary pain?

Rachel's kiss was a beautiful illustration of how we should respond to God during times of confusion and suffering. We struggle to realize the purpose of difficult circumstances. Yet God perfectly knows everything about the situation—what was, and is, and is to come—and about us and what we ultimately need. We are not a mystery to Him. As our Creator, He intimately knows every detail about us. He has complete understanding of every person and every situation. And He loves us with an everlasting love. So next time we're tempted to whine and complain, maybe instead we can offer a kiss of faith to our Lord, knowing He only allows what is ultimately right and kind in the lives of His children.

Sometimes I forget, Lord, that You are omniscient, You know all. Sometimes I forget that You understand everything about all that exists, has existed in the past, and will exist in the times to come, so You certainly understand me and my needs. Yet I'm still often met with confusion and frustration when difficult things assail me. Remind me, Lord, of Your perfect knowledge. You know what I need before I ask. You know the number of hairs on my head. You know when I sit and when I rise and what I will say before I speak

Sometimes I Forget

it. Help me remember that, as the Source and Author of all things, You know instantly and with a fullness of perfection all that can be known. Therefore, I can rest in Your discernment and action in my life. Help me trust in Your infinite knowledge and understanding.

TRUTH REMINDER
God perfectly knows it all, so He certainly knows what's best for me.

14: God Is Kind

Sometimes I forget, Lord, that You are *kind*, sympathetic and willing to help. . . .

> Or do you despise the riches of his kindness, restraint, and patience, not recognizing that God's kindness is intended to lead you to repentance? (Rom. 2:4)

"As we stand in awe of God—his love, kindness, and care—life loses any threat it might have held over us. Even when life seems out to get us, God is intent on saving us."
DERON SPOO[16]

Grabbing Rach, I tried to steer her around the man. She pulled her arm away, making a beeline for the unkempt individual sitting a couple of tables away.

"Hi," she quipped with her typical greeting. Her usual smile lit up her face, and to all the world, she looked like she had just met her best friend. He returned her greeting and smile, and before I could stop her, she bent in for a hug. The man's face beamed.

I stammered a quiet, "Have a nice day," as I finally managed to guide my daughter to the door of the restaurant.

"Rach, we can't hug total strangers," I began, a futile attempt to contain my daughter's love and kindness. Rachel has a bent toward others. She extends kindness in the form of smiles, greetings, and hugs to whomever she thinks needs it. Unkempt

Sometimes I Forget

diners in restaurants, smelly people on the street, or the sloppily dressed woman in the doctor's waiting room—Rachel is not confined to presupposed ideas of who she should be kind too. She's spontaneous in extending her gentle sympathy.

Like every other good character trait we possess, God authored kindness. He wrote it in our DNA when He created us in His image. And He perfectly and infinitely possesses and exercises kindness. But sometimes His kindness is not as obvious as Rachel's. Sometimes it doesn't look sympathetic or helpful at all. A closed door to an opportunity we had prayed for, an illness, even a death. God's kindness can and does at times look like suffering because we can't see all He does or His reasons behind it. In His omniscience, He perfectly knows what's best for us. Even an obvious hurt can be a hidden blessing when seen through His infinite, loving eyes.

Rachel extends kindness in an obvious manner, intent on bringing about a smile. God is perfectly kind. But He not only blesses us in extraordinary and apparent ways, He sometimes allows or orchestrates things that don't appear so kind to us. A parent delivering bitter medicine; a doctor breaking a bone to get it to properly mend; a friend tackling another to get them out of the way of an oncoming train; the death of Jesus on the cross—not all kind actions appear to be so. Because our infinitely loving, holy, just, powerful, and kind God isn't after our happiness and comfort as much as He is after our souls—wanting us with Him for eternity—as He works to transform us into a clearer image of His Son, He may extend a severe kindness to bring that about. In the end, then, all we experience becomes a gift in the hands of our Almighty Father.

Sometimes I forget, Lord, that You are kind, *sympathetic and willing to help. I forget that, in Your perfect kindness, You give blessings to those who follow You and those who don't yet bow their*

Sometimes I Forget

knees. Your heart is bent toward all Your children. And even in my rebellion and wickedness, You extend Your hand to me, offering provision where I deserve punishment, salvation where I deserve condemnation. Help me remember Your loving-kindness, Lord, and that Your kindness won't always be nice and pleasant. When all I see is darkness, Lord, remind me of the light You're holding for me, the providential help You are already providing. Help me readily accept Your severe kindness as You draw me nearer to You in Your infinite wisdom and perfect love.

TRUTH REMINDER
God's kindness never wanes, so even difficult things in my life become gifts in His hands.

15: God Is Merciful

Sometimes I forget, Lord, that You are *merciful*, offering pardon instead of just condemnation. . . .

> Therefore the LORD is waiting to show you mercy,
> and is rising up to show you compassion,
> for the LORD is a just God.
> All who wait patiently for him are happy.
> (Isa. 30:18)

"God's mercy is so great that you may sooner drain the sea of its water, or deprive the sun of its light, or make space too narrow, than diminish the great mercy of God."
CHARLES SPURGEON[17]

There wasn't much I could do but hold the sobbing woman, uncomfortably shifting from one foot to the other. This was out of my comfort zone, like way out in a different country. Standing in line to have our books autographed, I didn't expect the outpouring of this dear lady's emotions.

The Holy Spirit used the speaker's powerful, grace-laced, scripturally based message to convince this daughter of His undying love for her and His capacity to forgive. Her regret and shame about her lurid past mixed with deep relief and gratitude. Yet she struggled to accept the reality that, in Christ, she was truly free.

I felt awkward in that moment, but we all need to hear about the scandalous mercy of our Lord—a mercy that defies human understanding. Divine mercy poured out on sinners. So, I assured

Sometimes I Forget

her that no sin or sorrow is too great to escape God's mercy. I reminded her that God delivers love, mercy, and righteousness to His children in perfect proportions. I consoled her with the truth that, thanks to the sacrifice of Jesus Christ, the Father pardons us, holding back the judgment we deserve. These were words I needed to hear as well.

Because I sin. In the words of Paul, "I do not practice what I want to do, but I do what I hate" (Rom. 7:15b). And no matter how many times I fall to temptation, the Lord is there—not to point His finger, not to chastise me, but to pick me up and encourage me all over again. To offer forgiveness and another chance. To give me mercy. Just as He did with so many throughout Scripture: the adulteress of her lurid past (John 8), Peter of his betrayal of Jesus (John 21), and Saul of his horrible persecution of Christians in his early years (Acts 9).

They fell into sin, but God reached out His hand and offered them redemption. He didn't condone what they had done, but He did offer them His mercy in spite of their failings. He does the same for us in all of our wayward steps.

The Lord is infinitely merciful, offering all believers pardon day in and day out. He doesn't keep count of our mistakes and He doesn't wait for us to be cleaned up. We don't deserve His mercy. We deserve condemnation and judgment. But Jesus, our Savior, stepped up to take the wrath of God for us. He received the judgment that should have been on us. And that mercy? In Christ, it's new and it's ours every day.

> *Sometimes I forget, Lord, that You are* merciful, *offering pardon instead of just condemnation. I forget that in the midst of my sinful thoughts and choices, You hold back the judgment I deserve, restraining Your wrath and offering me forgiveness in its place. Oh, Lord, forgive this wretched soul! Remind me that my sinful*

actions don't disqualify me. Help me remember that, in Your great and perfect mercy, I am forgiven. Strengthen me to walk in that pardon, so I can be an effective vessel in Your hands. Embolden me to remind those around me of Your unmerited mercy that is new every day.

TRUTH REMINDER
In God's mercy, I am not disqualified
by my sinful thoughts and choices
but receive pardon in Christ.

16: God Is Faithful

Sometimes I forget, Lord, that You are *faithful*, trustworthy in all things. . . .

> God is not a man, that he might lie,
> or a son of man, that he might change his mind.
> Does he speak and not act,
> or promise and not fulfill? (Num. 23:19)

> *"Far above all finite comprehension is
> the unchanging faithfulness of God."*
> ARTHUR W. PINK[18]

Raised eyebrows met my confession. They spoke the question the ladies wouldn't utter: "How could you?" It was something I had asked myself more than once. How can any mother forget her child? And not only once, but three times. I'm supposed to be there for my children. To be a haven for them, trustworthy and certain. Instead, I had recently forgotten my youngest for the third time (this was the second time at church). In my defense, none of the times lasted more than a few minutes, but still . . . I failed the very person who depended on me most. (Not too scarred by these incidences, my son still delights in giving me a hard time about it.)

Thankfully, we have One who will never abandon nor forget us. In fact, God's faithfulness extends across all facets of our lives. He never wavers in fulfilling His promises, and He doesn't forget or change His mind depending on how He feels that day or what we've done. In His infinite love and holiness, the Lord remains the

Sometimes I Forget

One to trust. In Deuteronomy, we are assured that we serve "a faithful God, without bias, he is righteous and true" (32:4).

I love my children with all the love I possess, but still, I fail them. That's why I've been intentional to point them to the Lord. The most loving human in their lives, the most loving human in the life of anyone, will fail. We can count on it. But we can also count on and cling to throughout our lives that our God will never fail us. He loves fully, provides completely, and guides perfectly. We will fail, and we will be on the receiving end of someone's failing, so let's place our hope in God. He is the only One who is absolutely trustworthy.

Sometimes I forget, Lord, that You are faithful, trustworthy in all things. I forget that You never waver in Your loyalty but are always working in my life for my good. I know it, Lord. I've read about Your faithfulness and heard it preached many times, but when times grow difficult, I still doubt. In my loneliness, I wonder where You've been. In my pain, I question what You are doing and allowing. Remind me, dear Lord, of Your consistent and active presence in my life. Help me remember that You never fail, never forget, and never fall short. Assure me once again that what You say I can trust.

TRUTH REMINDER
God is forever faithful and will never fail me,
never forget me, and never fall short.

17: God Is Triune

Sometimes I forget, Lord, that You are *triune*, one entity with three persons. . . .

> The grace of the Lord Jesus Christ, and the love of God, and the fellowship of the Holy Spirit be with you all. (2 Cor. 13:13)

"The mystery at the epicenter of the universe—namely, the triune being of God—is also the heart of our salvation. Our redemption is Trinitarian in its structure."
PHILIP RYKEN AND MICHAEL LEFEBVRE[19]

The sky glowed azure. The packed snow gleamed dazzling white as far as the eye could see in a vast tundra-like area. Squinting against the reflecting sun, I walked with my family over a narrow, snow-covered, arched earth bridge. The kids moved ahead, dragging their saucers and sleds. Laughter rang in the air as the boys and my husband slid the afternoon away as Rachel and I explored the landscape on our feet.

As twilight approached, I quieted Rach and listened intently in the deafening silence. With heightening alarm, I realized we could no longer hear the guys. Apparently, we had gotten way ahead of them. Scanning the horizon revealed they were nowhere in sight.

Evening was approaching. The sky darkening. Night fell quickly over the vast frozen sea. I looked back. Oddly, I could make out our footprints on the bridge we had crossed hours ago, but no one was there either. Rach and I found ourselves alone. I became frantic. "Dave!" "Danny!" "Zach!" "Joey!"

Out of nowhere, the boys came zipping over the bridge and past us on their saucers, having a blast. I couldn't see my husband, but in that moment it wasn't a concern. We were no longer alone, and that brought great solace. This vivid dream left me thinking about being in relationship with God.

We welcome a bit of quiet in the midst of hectic days, but for most of us, being alone in an unfamiliar and isolating situation is concerning. We appreciate having a familiar face nearby. As Father, Son, and Holy Spirit, each person of the Trinity has always been in fellowship. Created in the Triune God's image, it's only natural, then, that we find comfort in community. God has been in relationship from infinity and desires a relationship with each of us. A profound mystery, each personality is truly, fully, and completely God, but each has unique roles. We reflect the roles of each in the way we represent the Father's mercy, the Son's sacrifice, and the Holy Spirit's power, and the three persons cooperate in the work of our salvation.

While we can never fully comprehend the Trinity, we can gain in understanding and awe of our tri-personal God. We can begin to better understand how He works in our salvation and the place of fellowship in our lives. And we can take solace in the fact that no matter how lonely we feel, we will never be alone. We have the three-in-one God watching over us and working in and through us, and we have fellow believers encouraging and coming alongside us. So even if we find ourselves alone and isolated in a vast tundra, we can be comforted. We were born into relationship.

Sometimes I forget, Lord, that You are triune, *one entity with three persons. I forget that You dwelt in community from eternity, one substance expressed in three personalities. Therefore, it's only natural that being created in Your image, relationship holds great meaning for me as Your child. Remind me that Your tri-personal nature does cooperative work in my life in many ways, including the work completed for my salvation. You made me worthy to be in Your presence forever as Your redeemed child. Strengthen my faith in You and my understanding of You as Father, Son, and Holy Spirit. Remind me that I never need fear being alone because You worked in Your persons to be in relationship with me. And help me remember, Lord, that I belong to a much bigger community in the family of believers.*

TRUTH REMINDER
The cooperative work of the triune God has secured a relationship with me for all eternity and created me to be in community with other believers.

18: God Is Simple

Sometimes I forget, Lord, that You are *simple*, one essence and unified, undivided in nature and in actions. . . .

> "Listen, Israel: The LORD our God, the LORD is one." (Deut. 6:4)

". . . neither You nor Your eternity which You are have parts, no part of You or of Your eternity is anywhere or at any time, but You exist as a whole everywhere and Your eternity exists as a whole always."
ANSELM OF CANTERBURY[20]

"Julie, this is Jeannie."

I froze, my cell phone pressed to my ear. *No, not now. Not yet!* But I already knew. Nothing more needed to be said. With those four words, I knew my much-needed respite week would end prematurely.

The camp program director continued: "Rachel's having difficulty. She's shoving others and won't do anything we ask her to. Another camper is scared to be around her. Any ideas?"

No! No ideas! This is your job. I'm done. This is my one week off. I wanted to scream those words to the wonderful lady on the other end. Instead, I offered what ideas I had and then tried to talk Rach through her behaviors. We hung up. Jeannie and the counselors hopeful. Me defeated. Even the crackling fire my husband later kindled under a clear, calm night couldn't restore the peace stolen by our brief conversation.

Sometimes I Forget

Rachel (our precious young-adult daughter who functions on the level of a preschooler) was off to an amazing camp for five nights, our oldest boys no longer lived at home, and our youngest was working at church camp for the week. My husband and I had a rare five days to ourselves. After working for a couple of them, we would have three wonderful days to relax and focus on our relationship.

And it proved itself to be everything I needed . . . for a far-too-short time period. Then the dreaded call came, and the stress I managed to set aside for an entire glorious twenty-four hours came rushing back. *Why, Lord? A few days to renew and refresh. That's all I'm asking for!*

The next morning dawned with another call, followed by a silent drive to camp to pick up our daughter—three days early. I was crushed.

Sometimes it seems God isn't very caring or understanding. Sometimes things seem unfair. If all things flow through God's sphere of influence before they get to us, why doesn't He make them better? Was I asking too much in seeking a bit of rest? Was God punishing me for something? Was He ignoring my needs, or didn't He care?

When we face hard things in life, it's common to question God and His goodness, kindness, justice, and love. We hurt, and we know He can help. But it's important we remember the Lord's unified, simple nature. God is One, completely integrated, infinitely perfect in who He is. In other words, His attributes work in perfect harmony. One never "outweighs" another. Every attribute is completely true of God and His character. There isn't one more important than another. God is as much in control and righteous as He is gracious and merciful. He is entirely just, entirely loving, entirely kind, and entirely holy.

Not just even-balanced, God's attributes are all integrated in His very being. So we can trust Him completely and fully. We

Sometimes I Forget

can turn to Him with our struggles, frustrations, heartaches, and pains. We can go to Him to exchange the weight of the world for His light yoke (Matt. 11:28–30). We can let Him fill us up with just what we need. And we can count on Him for eternal life. In light of God's simplicity, we can count on all He is to be good news to us.

Sometimes I forget, Lord, that You are simple, one essence and unified, undivided in nature and in actions. I forget that one of Your attributes doesn't outweigh another. They are integrated in your very being. Remind me, Lord, that Your love isn't at the exclusion of Your justice, Your grace doesn't act separately from Your holiness. You are fully all You are, and You interact with us as such. I struggle to understand and accept such a magnificent concept, Lord, but remind me that I can trust all You are to be good news to me.

TRUTH REMINDER
In God's simplicity, His one essence,
all He is, is good news to me.

19: God Is Wise

Sometimes I forget, Lord, that You are *wise*, always knowing and acting in a way that is best. . . .

> Oh, the depth of the riches
> and the wisdom and the knowledge of God!
> How unsearchable his judgments
> and untraceable his ways! (Rom. 11:33)

*"A God wise enough to create me and the world
I live in is wise enough to watch out for me."*
PHILIP YANCEY[21]

Tears threatened to spill as my husband and then my oldest read from their gratitude leaves. At Thanksgiving, everyone in our family jots down on paper leaves five things from the past year that they're grateful for. One year was particularly poignant. It had been a difficult year of seemingly missed opportunities for two in our family. My husband had put in for a supervisor position but was turned down. Our oldest son took two hits over the year: He had applied to be a floor residence assistant for his dorm but didn't get it, and at the beginning of the year, he asked for certain work hours and was disappointed to be assigned less and different hours. I remember the frustration and confusion I felt for them at the time. However, later that year both of them realized the blessing of not getting what they had originally wanted.

That's the thing about God. He doesn't always answer our prayers the way we want Him to at the time, but He always

Sometimes I Forget

answers with what's best for us. The Lord is consistently and infinitely wise. He possesses complete discernment and knowledge. He has perfect, unchanging wisdom. He is always doing the wisest thing in our lives. So His "no" or "not this" are exactly what we need (although not always want we want).

Unfulfilled expectations lead to great disappointment. We can let go of those expectations when we remember that God knows what's best and only gives us what's ultimately good for us. Since wisdom is part of God's very being and He guides our lives, we can feel certain the path He directs us to is the perfect one for us. God only allows or orchestrates in our lives the wisest things.

Sometimes I forget, Lord, that You are wise, always knowing and acting in a way that is best. I forget that Your complete knowledge and discernment perfectly direct my steps. So I doubt You when You answer my prayers differently than I'd like. Remind me, Lord, that You only and always want what is ultimately best for me. Help me remember that You act in complete harmony with Your wisdom. You choose wisely on my behalf and answer my prayers in accordance with what You perfectly know. Assure me that You are always working in my life. Help me trust that my circumstances are always, in some way, the best for me, because You care too much for me to give me anything less.

TRUTH REMINDER
Every moment of every day God is doing
the wisest thing in my life.

20: God Is Holy

Sometimes I forget, Lord, that You are *holy*, divinely perfect and set apart from all evil and sin. . . .

> Each of the four living creatures had six wings;
> they were covered with eyes around and inside.
> Day and night they never stop, saying,
>
> > Holy, holy, holy,
> > Lord God, the Almighty,
> > who was, who is, and who is to come.
>
> (Rev. 4:8)

"The most damnable and pernicious heresy that has ever plagued the mind of man was the idea that somehow he could make himself good enough to deserve to live with an all-holy God."

MARTIN LUTHER[22]

No one knows for sure why my husband's great-grandfather left. Times were hard, no doubt; the turn of the twentieth century wasn't easy for many. But still . . .

Perhaps he felt there was more to life. Maybe he thought real adventure lay somewhere other than the Wisconsin farm he shared with his wife and children. Or maybe he left to pursue fame and fortune.

No matter the reason, his traveling took him to the state of Washington. During the following decade his family received a few letters. It was obvious from his writing that life wasn't rosy in the Northwest either.

Sometimes I Forget

Years later the family heard the final word. The wandering husband and father had died—apparently tragically, apparently alone.

What prompted a father to forsake his children? What drove a man to leave behind loved ones and all that is familiar for an unknown land? What kept him away when faced with a lonely, desperate life?

Pride, greed, selfishness . . . in a word, *sin*. We all suffer from it in our fallen nature, our old Adam, and it separates us from the gifts our heavenly Father desires for us. But God, in His abundant mercy, provides a better way, one that doesn't end in separation and death.

Unlike us, God is sinless, only doing what is right and just and loving. In fact, He hates sin and charges us to live holy lives too: "He has told you, O man, what is good; and what does the Lord require of you but to do justice, and to love kindness, and to walk humbly with your God?" (Mic. 6:8 ESV). But in His foreknowledge, He's aware that we'll fall short—from the foolish teenager to the most learned Bible scholar. So mercifully, God sent a Savior for all of mankind. Jesus Christ, born of a virgin, suffered and died to justify and redeem us from condemnation and our sins. In Christ, God forgives us all our sins.

That's not all though. To be righteous, we need to perfectly walk in holiness; an impossibility as beings born in sin. We disobey, rebel, and turn away when we live out of our old Adam. But what a beautiful and comforting truth to know we are not left there. God sent the Holy Spirit to sanctify us, bringing us to faith and directing and empowering us to live a godly life.

Without the gift of salvation, you and I are lost in our sins. We can't be or act holy without the finished work of Jesus Christ and the indwelling of the Holy Spirit. So our holy God extends mercy to us, clothing us with a holiness we cannot earn. By His grace, forgiven and saved unto eternity, we can join the angels in

Sometimes I Forget

glorifying our Holy God, boldly proclaiming: "Holy, holy, holy, is the Lord God Almighty" (Rev. 4:8 NIV)!

Sometimes I forget, Lord, that You are holy, *divinely perfect and set apart from all evil and sin. I forget that, without your gift of holiness, I cannot even be in Your presence. Remind me of Your mercy in offering the free gift of salvation to me and all of Your people. Remind me of the forgiveness I receive in Christ Jesus and that by His death and resurrection He redeems me. Thank You, Lord, for sending Your Spirit to sanctify me, growing faith in me and empowering me to live an increasingly holy life. Help me walk as one redeemed instead of as one condemned.*

TRUTH REMINDER
God saved me from my sins
through the blood of Jesus Christ
and continues to grow faith in me.

21: God Is Gracious

Sometimes I forget, Lord, that You are *gracious*, pronouncing favor where there should be punishment. . . .

> For you are saved by grace through faith, and this is not from yourselves; it is God's gift—not from works, so that no one can boast. (Eph. 2:8–9)

"Grace is the delivery of a jewel that nobody ordered, a burst of light in a room where everyone forgot it was dark."
DAVID JEREMIAH[23]

Growing up, us six kids would exchange Christmas gifts by drawing names and buying for that one person. We usually shared lists so we'd get something we wanted. Christmas Eve was exchange night. I loved the anticipation as we waited our turn to unwrap our gift(s). One year when I was in high school, an older brother drew my name. Around Thanksgiving, I carefully scripted a list that included those few things I really wanted. For weeks this brother threatened to give me a rock and a stick. I wouldn't let him get to me, so I joked that I could really use those, confident he was just teasing. To my shock, that Christmas Eve I did, indeed, unwrap a rock and a stick.

My brother didn't leave me there though. Later that day, he graced me with a wonderful gift, an album from one of my favorite singers (John Denver), and what appeared to be a mean gesture became a favorite memory.

Sometimes I Forget

A rock and a stick. More fair, a lump of coal. As mean as that sounds as a gift, it would be far too great of a present for God to give us. In our disobedience, we deserve only judgment. What claim do we have on the One who created us and controls the entire universe? How many of us love unconditionally, serve our neighbor perfectly, or entertain only holy thoughts like He commanded? Not one! In one of his psalms, King David wrote: "All have turned away; all alike have become corrupt. There is no one who does good, not even one" (Ps. 14:3).

Unless we carry out all of God's attributes perfectly, we fail in the goodness department and are not deserving of heaven. But every human on the planet is steeped in sin from birth. Nothing we can do will ever be enough to overcome our sin. Therefore, it's humanly impossible to be good. A discouraging thought? It could be and should be if one doesn't know Jesus Christ as their Lord and Savior. God knew we were lost in our sin, but He has such intense love for each of us that He sent to us the greatest gift, a gift that changed everything: saving grace in the form of an infant.

Like the Christmas gift of the rock and a stick I received those many years ago, we don't always get what we want in this broken world. Although He would be justified in leaving us alone in our suffering, God loves us too deeply. So, in His abundant and sufficient grace, He works together all things we receive for some good purpose (Rom. 8:28)—in this world and ultimately in the next. And as we continue to unwrap the gift of surrendered faith, some of what looks to be mean and ugly in our lives transforms into precious gifts that stretch, grow, and heal us. When we recognize the grace in our lives, we see abundant reason to thank God for His unmerited favor, even when we're left with a rock and a stick.

Sometimes I Forget

Sometimes I forget, Lord, that You are gracious, pronouncing favor where there should be punishment. I forget that, in Your perfect love, You freely give good and abundant gifts. I fall into the trap of trying to earn Your love, trying to prove my worthiness, or trying to be enough for all I'm facing. When I'm discouraged, please remind me of the plethora of common blessings You pour out on the world: the rain and sunshine, the miracle of new life, and plentiful daily provisions. Remind me of Your precious saving grace You give to all believers: the wiping away of our sins and the promise of eternal life. I am not worthy, Lord, yet You give me faith, and in Christ, You forgive me and sustain me. And help me remember, Lord, that I don't have to do this life or this walk of faith on my own, but that You are my Sustainer and Perfecter. Thank You for Your unmerited, all-sufficient grace.

TRUTH REMINDER
God pours out blessings when
what I deserve is judgment.

22: God Is Attentive

Sometimes I forget, Lord, that You are *attentive*, perfectly offering intercession and support. . . .

> This is the confidence we have before him: If we ask anything according to his will, he hears us. And if we know that he hears whatever we ask, we know that we have what we have asked of him. (1 John 5:14–15)

"You always have God's undivided attention."
CHARLES STANLEY[24]

As I rushed to check the "to dos" off my list, I heard it. A single word that floated down the hall: "Mama." My daughter spoke it so softly and sweetly, the only name she's ever used for me. It squeezed under her bedroom door and found me. And I responded. How could I not? She is my daughter whom I love. When Rachel reaches out to me, I respond.

Like any good parent, I'm attentive to the calls of my children. I may not always respond the way they'd like, but I do draw near to hear their request or problem. And I do pay attention to their concerns and actions. The Bible says God also is an attentive parent. Only He does it perfectly. He perfectly pays attention to His children. He perfectly hears our call. He perfectly sees our actions. He perfectly notices the happenings in our lives. Even more, the Holy Spirit intercedes with the Father on our behalf,

Sometimes I Forget

giving our groanings meaning and making our requests known (Rom. 8:26–27).

It's startling to think that the God of the universe pays attention to little ole me. It becomes more stunning to realize He hears and sees the prayers and concerns of all whom He created in His image. Not only that, but He has His hand on the rest of creation too, sustaining and maintaining it. Our Lord has a lot to juggle. He keeps the world spinning while giving us all the attention we need. And you think you're busy!

My daughter knows I will come when she calls my name . . . if I hear her. But I'm not always around or near enough. We don't have to worry about that with God. Whenever and wherever we need Him, He is there. Before we even reach out to God, we've arrested His attention. He always hears and sees at the time we need Him to. A simple prayer and He draws near. A groan and His gaze is upon us. A misstep and He's aware. We don't need to wax elegant. Our words don't have to take on a certain cadence or follow a specific protocol. Our actions don't have to be extravagant.

Although we have good intentions, we will never be perfectly attentive and responsive to those in our care. But we can trust that God is. It's in His very nature. He not only delights in us, His children, but He is ever aware of all our needs and desires. God won't be sleeping, absent, or tuned in elsewhere when we have a need. He is flawlessly attentive and will always respond in a like manner. We can count on it!

Sometimes I forget, Lord, that You are attentive, *perfectly offering intercession and support. I forget that You are never asleep, never absent, and never tuned in elsewhere. Remind me that, in Your magnificence and mysteriousness, You are fully attuned to each of us and all of us. Remind me that I'm not alone in my needs. You sent Your Spirit to help me—strengthening, guiding, and interceding. When I don't know what to pray, the Holy Spirit will interpret my groans. Help me remember, Lord, that You delight in me and are ever aware of my needs and desires. Thank You for always noticing me and always providing what I need.*

TRUTH REMINDER
God is ever attentive to me as His child,
always hearing my cries and praises.

23: God Is Glorious

Sometimes I forget, Lord, that You are *glorious*, infinitely beautiful and great. . . .

> Then the glory of the Lord rose from above the cherub to the threshold of the temple. The temple was filled with the cloud, and the court was filled with the brightness of the Lord's glory. (Ezek. 10:4)

"Glorious the song, when God's the theme."
CHRISTOPHER SMART[25]

Her twinkling eyes catch the glimmer of the raindrop as it strikes the glass. "Hi!" She greets it as if an old friend. She grins and giggles over what appears to be much of nothing but which really might be everything. Her joy is infectious. She includes everyone in her circle. Bear hugs and hand-holdings all around. She welcomes the moon whenever it dares to make its appearance. And the sun? It gets noticed as soon as it peaks its first rays above the horizon or around the clouds.

My daughter attacks her days with an attention to detail that is astonishing, yet with a generality that leaves little out. And how do I go about my days? If I'm honest, it's often with groaning and moaning. As I'm scrubbing the toilet, I wonder: What is it all about? What is the purpose of one more day of food preparation and child bathing and clothes folding and going to work and lending a listening ear? It all repeats in a dizzying manner.

Sometimes I Forget

Where is the glory in this? The truth is, apart from God, there is no meaning in what is being done on this spinning earth; there is no glory. If done just to do it, all is meaningless. For it will all pass away. If our only concern is addressing the temporal and ignoring the eternal, then real meaning doesn't exist.

But the Lord is glorious. His splendor and beauty are unsurpassed. God's glory is so splendid it fills creation. This ground we walk on was made with holy hands. As we walk out His divine plan for our lives, it's on holy ground. As we work for Christ, it's all hallowed. God makes it all meaningful. The scrubbing, the folding, the hugging, the laughing, and the crying. It's all worth it if done in the context of forever. If done in service to the Lord in Holy reverence.

God created us in His image to reflect His glory, in how we conduct ourselves, in what we do with our days. The apostle Paul tells us that we "are being transformed into his image with ever-increasing glory" (2 Cor. 3:18 NIV). As we go about our days, doing His will in obedience and reverence, we reflect His glory, the beauty of who He is. We become more Christ-like, a more radiant reflection. We have even more glory awaiting us though! Through the atoning blood of Jesus, we've been adopted by God, grafted into His family, and as children of the King, we will inherit and inhabit the new earth and new heaven. What grandeur to look forward to!

So instead of looking at our days with dread, let's move into them with awe and reverence and wonder. Let's welcome the storms of life as a chance to grow in our faith, to reflect the beauty and splendor of God more clearly. And let's glory in the most amazing gift of all: an eternity in the presence of our Lord as heirs to His kingdom.

Sometimes I Forget

Sometimes I forget, Lord, that You are glorious, infinitely beautiful and great. I forget that Your radiance and splendor emanate from all that You are and all that You do and are seen in all of creation. Forgive me, Lord, when I let circumstances blur my reflection, when I try to soldier through without acknowledging that You are in it all. Remind me that You infuse meaning and beauty in my difficult and mundane days when I surrender them to You. Help me remember that others see You in me, and help me reflect Your splendor by walking in obedience and reverence. May You be glorified in my actions and words.

TRUTH REMINDER
God created me to reflect His glory, His beauty and His splendor, and I do so through obedience and reverence.

24: God Is Patient

Sometimes I forget, Lord, that You are *patient*, long-suffering and restraining. . . .

> The Lord does not delay his promise, as some understand delay, but is patient with you, not wanting any to perish but all to come to repentance. (2 Pet. 3:9)

"Restlessness and impatience change nothing except our peace and joy. Peace does not dwell in outward things, but in the heart prepared to wait trustfully and quietly on Him who has all things safely in His hands."

ELISABETH ELLIOT[26]

With head down, I slumped through the snow, my husband trailing behind. We entered the barn and Dave explained what he needed me for.

"It shouldn't take more than ten minutes," he assured me.

I glanced at my watch, trying to control the panic rising in me. I couldn't help it; ten minutes was ten minutes I did not have. *I'll be up late again. I can never catch up or get ahead. And I'm never going to get my book written on time.* Negative thoughts kept up a steady march through my head.

With mounting anxiety, I watched the ten minutes become thirty. My flesh screamed to hurry, to nag and complain to my husband. Ferociously tamping down my agitation, I grabbed at a thought that flitted by—a teaching by Elisabeth

Sometimes I Forget

Elliott—"Restlessness and impatience change nothing except our peace and joy." I could vouch for that! My peace and joy had long since left me and my impatience hadn't helped anything.

Waiting and enduring patiently has never been a strong suit of mine, and it's still a weakness despite the Lord giving me plenty of opportunities to practice patience. But God, He demonstrates great patience with His children. Repeatedly, the Israelites turned to complaining in the wake of a mercy from God. Manna, quail, water. No sooner would they receive their fill then they would renew their grumbling.

Repeatedly, I give into impatience and restlessness as well. With abundant blessings surrounding me, I mutter about what I don't have, whether it is time to complete a task or a desired object or outcome. Just like the Israelites did after God rescued them from Egypt, I get amnesia quickly and often, forgetting all He has done for me. I can't go a measly half hour without complaining.

This stirs in me increased amazement at the Lord's great patience and extended long-suffering. He doesn't want any to perish, so with abundant restraint, He endures faithlessness by His children while demonstrating His mercy and pouring out His grace. He puts up with our apathy, our idolatry, our doubt for a measure of time far beyond what is reasonable and justified. And He provides opportunities for us to grow in patience, situations for us to practice waiting and enduring, like my trudge to the barn. So instead of a grumbling nature, we should ask the Lord for His patience. In gratitude for His long-suffering, we can learn to extend mercy and grace to those in our lives that interrupt and let us down. We can surrender our impatience as an expression of our trust in the Lord. As a forgiven and redeemed child, waiting on His perfect timing in whatever we face will give us the perfect opportunity to grow in our own faith and to be conduits of His love and grace to those He's still seeking after. The Lord

Sometimes I Forget

is infinitely patient with us. May we grow to reflect a bit of that in our own days.

> *Sometimes I forget, Lord, that You are patient, long-suffering and restraining. I forget that You want none to perish, so You extend mercy and grace far beyond what is reasonable and justified. You often allow unwanted situations as opportunities for Your children to grow in faith and reflect You more clearly. Yet in my humanness, I quickly become impatient and restless, demanding action and resisting change. Thank You for enduring my childishness, my petulance, as I repeatedly grumble. Thank You for putting up with my apathy, idolatry, and doubt. Remind me of how often You forgive me. Help me surrender my impatience, trusting in Your perfect timing. Help me to see in my difficulties opportunities to grow in patience. And help me, dear Lord, be a conduit for Your love and grace, reaching out to those for whom You wait so patiently.*

TRUTH REMINDER
The Lord's timing is perfect, patiently giving me opportunities to grow in faith and share the Good News with others.

25: God Is Impeccable

Sometimes I forget, Lord, that You are *impeccable*, incapable of sinning and entirely without fault or flaw. . . .

> For we do not have a high priest who is unable to sympathize with our weaknesses, but one who has been tempted in every way as we are, yet without sin. (Heb. 4:15)

". . . because the Lord Jesus is Almighty, having absolute power over sin, the feeble and sorely-tried saint may turn to Him in implicit confidence, seeking His efficacious aid. Only He who triumphed over sin, both in life and in death, can save me from my sins."

ARTHUR W. PINK[27]

"You did it on purpose!" The words shot from my mouth, projected through lips squashed into a tight line. Hot tears stung my cheeks. I was certain he didn't care. I wanted to make him.

For months I'd nursed a weeping willow sapling, hoping to transplant it to a more permanent home in our lawn. I love the graceful waves of branches on the full-grown tree. My husband only sees the mess those branches make.

Nevertheless, my sons and I had climbed an adult willow, pruned off a branch, sprouted roots in water, and planted it in our sheltered nursery garden.

With eagerness, I'd watched it cling to life and finally take off. Soon, I'd be able to transplant it. However, as I mowed around the

Sometimes I Forget

small nursery garden that day, I noticed my little willow was gone, obviously struck down by a weed whip.

I knew my husband had weed-whipped that morning. I knew he didn't like the tree. I *knew* he whipped it down on purpose.

With each round on the mower, my anger grew. Ugly thoughts of past hurts bubbled to the surface, being relived in my self-righteous mind. Certain my vehemency was justified, I glared at my husband as he smiled at me from the tractor.

Confused, my long-suffering man finally demanded an explanation for the daggers I was shooting in his direction. I took full advantage of the opportunity, determined to make him feel my fury. Only in the end, I had to sheepishly retract my words as he assured me he would never purposely do such a thing. He hadn't even seen the little tree among the tall grass that surrounded it.

This isn't the first time I've had to eat my words. Often I blurt before I speak, only to be frantically stuffing the words back in a split second later. (Which doesn't work, by the way.) My pride and self-righteousness get the better of me. My feelings get hurt, and I hurt in return. I think I've been wronged and justify my wrong words. I replay the past infractions against me and let those destructive thoughts simmer for a while, stirring them up with righteous spices that proclaim my worth, until finally, the brew can be contained no longer. It bubbles out from under the lid, full of steam, and burns whomever it comes in contact with. Oh, to have a lock on that lid!

I'm ashamed of my sin. I'd like to wipe it out. But the truth is everyone has inherited a sinful nature. And we'll continue to sin until we go to our heavenly home. But we have good news, incomprehensibly wonderful news: We have a Father who loves us to such a great depth He gave up His Son to take away our sins, every last one of them! But that's only possible because of our triune God's impeccable nature. Father, Son, and Holy Spirit had to be incapable of sinning to take away our transgressions. We needed a spotless Lamb to be sacrificed for our sins in our stead, a flawless Intercessor to pay the price for our offenses. Thanks be to God, we have that in Jesus Christ, the incarnate Son of God.

As fully man, Jesus faced many temptations. As fully God, He perfectly resisted those temptations. But equally important and mind-boggling is that the fully man/fully God being was incapable of sinning. Arthur W. Pink, in "The Impeccability of Christ," explains it this way: "while the Mediator was commissioned to die (John 10:18), He was not commissioned to sin. The human nature of Christ was permitted to function freely and normally: hence it wearied and wept; but to sin is not a normal act of human nature."[28] In order to aid us in our afflictions, our Redeemer had to have the power to overcome all sin.

The Lord is sinless, even incapable of sinning. As immutable, unchanging, He always has been and always will be. He gets angry, but it's righteous. He punishes, but it's just. He never makes mistakes or responds out of character. God is always as He is.

Because the incarnate Son of God remained sinless, He became the unblemished Lamb needed to atone for our sins. No one else would be spotless. No one else would measure up. Without the sinless nature of Jesus Christ, you and I would still be lost in our sin. What a glorious God! What a glorious gift!

Sometimes I forget, Lord, that You are impeccable, incapable of sinning and entirely without fault or flaw. I forget that my sins are covered by Your sinlessness. I beat myself up over my transgressions. I am tempted to wallow in my unrighteousness. But that would be dismissing all You did for me on the cross. Remind me, Lord, of Your great love for me, of Your substitutionary atonement for my sins in the life and death of Jesus Christ, the spotless Lamb.

Sometimes I Forget

Remind me that in His inability to transgress, His overcoming of temptation, and His ultimate defeat of sin and death lie my salvation. I don't have to do any more. It is finished!

TRUTH REMINDER
The Lord is incapable of sinning, so in Christ, I can be confident in my salvation. It is finished!

26. God Is Jealous

Sometimes I forget, Lord, that You are *jealous*, not wanting to share your children's allegiance. . . .

> "For the LORD your God is a consuming fire, a jealous God." (Deut. 4:24)

> *"Hold everything in your hands lightly,*
> *otherwise it hurts when God pries your fingers open."*
> CORRIE TEN BOOM[29]

Life as a parent is interesting. You spend the first twelve years of a child's life holding them close and then the rest of their life letting them go. In the throes of the early years, holding them close and directing their steps can seem daunting. But I'm finding the latter years far harder. Releasing them from the nest has tested my obedience and stretched my heart.

Although written about an entirely different aspect, Andrew Budek-Schmeisser, a blogger whose life is slowly being taken by cancer, has some interesting thoughts about letting go:

> Ownership is the thing that makes dying hard. I think of Barb, the dogs, the house, and my very life as mine, and it feels like they're being taken from me. But if I willingly let go, surrendering them all to the God whose they are in the first place, I'm not stepping back from love.

Sometimes I Forget

> I can love all the more, because my heart is not
> clogged with a desperate greed.[30]

Surrendering . . . letting go. It seems that's the most difficult part of dying. Honestly, I think that's the most difficult part of living. We desire control. We thrive on believing we know best. We like the title of owner. Yet whether we're living or dying, just beginning our family or clutching the hem of our children's shirts as they stretch their wings and begin to fly, we must remember our place as stewards. God loaned us His children to raise. They are His . . . first and always. The same can be said and should be realized about all we possess. Our spouse. Our wealth. Our health. God owns it all, graciously loaning it to us for a season. When we forget that, we're making an idol of what we hold so tightly. A practice expressly forbidden. In fact, God wrote it in stone in the Ten Commandments, so the Israelites, and now we, wouldn't forget it. Exodus 34:14 (ESV) clearly states: "for you shall worship no other god, for the Lord, whose name is Jealous, is a jealous God."

We are the Lord's; all of creation belongs to Him. And He rightly insists on our total passion and affection. So, when our devotion shifts to another person or thing, He moves to draw us back. As God's beloved children, He gives us many good gifts. But we belong to Him, and He alone is worthy of our ultimate allegiance and honor. Whether it's children, possessions, or a position, let's ask the Lord to help us surrender them to Him, placing them in the proper order in our lives. It's then we'll find true joy and peace in our blessings.

Sometimes I forget, Lord, that You are jealous, *not wanting to share your children's allegiance. I forget that I am Yours and Yours alone, and I am to worship You and You alone. Forgive me when I turn my affections away from You. Remind me, Lord, that all*

Sometimes I Forget

I have is on loan from You. Help me remember to hold the good gifts You give loosely—my loved ones, my possessions, my work—and to turn to You with my allegiance. Help me find joy and peace in surrendering all I hold dear to You, a sacrifice of devotion to the only One worthy. Direct my heart to You, Lord, as the One who truly fulfills me.

TRUTH REMINDER
Everything belongs to God; He alone is worthy of my ultimate allegiance and devotion.

27. God Is Protective

Sometimes I forget, Lord, that You are *protective*, providing rest and security. . . .

> God is our refuge and strength,
> a helper who is always found
> in times of trouble. (Ps. 46:1)

> *"We are secured not because we hold tightly*
> *to Jesus, but because he holds tightly to us."*
>
> R. C. SPROUL[31]

A precious little girl sat across the aisle from me, at the opposite window. No more than eight years old, she chattered endlessly to the mother-like woman next to her.

Little seemed to bother this young lady until the plane began to roll away from the gate. Then without hesitation, she grabbed the hand of her guardian. "I'm not afraid!" she declared, yet she maintained a firm grip on the hand offered until we were safely in the air.

What a wise little girl! When uncertainty enters our world, we need a hand to hold. Someone to assure us that all will be fine. Even if we can proclaim, "I'm not afraid!" it is still a comfort to know we have someone that cares holding onto us . . . just in case.

Not all of us have a motherly type we can grab onto, but we all have someone who will readily hold us. That someone is the One who "knew you" before time began, who stitched you together in your mother's womb (Jer. 1:5; Ps. 139:13 ESV). Our Lord possesses the power to create all of life, to calm the winds and waves with a word, to hang the sun and moon, and to breathe life into dust. He loves us so deeply He sent His Son to die for our sins. He cares enough to offer rest to all who are weary. He is the One who is willing to forgive every sin and redeem every hurt.

On the sixth day of creation, God looked at us, His children created in His image, and it was "very good" (Gen. 1:31). And then we sinned, and our Father kicked us out of the garden. To punish us? Perhaps partly, but ultimately to protect us from living forever in our sin-state. As His beloved, He knew that would be too much for us to bear. So He provided the ultimate solution. He put in a plan that would eventually restore us fully to Him, but in the meantime, one that provided for our protection from His wrath and the evil of Satan.

Our Lord is a protective God. A loving Father, He certainly offers daily help for our earthly life. In fact, at times I wonder how many harmful things He has protected me from, events and circumstances I will never know about this side of heaven. How many times has He sheltered me with His hand, like He did for Moses (Exod. 33:22)? How often has He led me away from certain disaster like He did for Lot (Genesis 19)? How frequently does He stop a car from hitting me, kill the errant cell in my body, or redirect my path from certain destruction?

God is loving, trustworthy, and protective, our refuge during our scariest moments and during those harmful times we aren't even aware of. Like the little girl in the airplane, you and I have a hand to hold: God's hand. Take it. Don't worry, He won't let go. He will provide us with rest and strength. He offers us shelter from earth's storms, a rock to stand on when the winds hit, an anchor when rough waters threaten to pull us under, and a shield to deflect the enemy's poisonous darts. And in His hands rest all the security we could ever ask for: the guarantee of a lifetime with

Sometimes I Forget

Him, a lifetime free of all pain and sorrow. That's security we cannot find in anyone else. That's security that can carry us through all the uncertainties of life. So go ahead, take His hand. He'll lead You through this life right into eternity.

Sometimes I forget, Lord, that You are protective, *providing rest and security to all who turn to You. Because I sometimes feel alone and overwhelmed in my circumstances, I forget that You are with me and walk with me through all life's storms. When I feel assaulted from all sides, remind me, Lord, that as a loving Father, You provide for my best and protect me from the rest. Remind me that whenever I am fearful I can run to you. Help me remember that You shield me from the enemy's poisonous darts when I don't even know I need shielding, that You provide me with shelter before I'm aware of the need for it. Thank You for being my refuge on earth, and thank You most of all, Lord, for Your protective love that delivered me from sin and reestablished my right relationship with You for eternity.*

TRUTH REMINDER
God perfectly provides for my best
and protects me from the rest.

28. God Is Transcendent

Sometimes I forget, Lord, that You are *transcendent*, unbound and distinct from any other being. . . .

> "For my thoughts are not your thoughts
> and your ways are not my ways."
>
> This is the LORD's declaration.
>
> "For as heaven is higher than earth,
> so my ways are higher than your ways,
> and my thoughts than your thoughts."
> (Isa. 55:8–9)

> *"The riddles of God are more satisfying*
> *than the solutions of man."*
>
> G. K. CHESTERTON[32]

Sara Frankl had a chronic, debilitating, painful disease that was slowly killing her. She spent years confined to her tiny apartment, unable to even venture outside because the air was poison to her.

Although there were many days she writhed in pain, "Gitzen Girl," as her family and close friends nicknamed her, didn't spend her days writhing in bitterness. Instead, she chose to bless instead of despair. She chose to praise instead of complain. She turned to technology to reach beyond the four walls of her home and impact thousands of others. She became a joyful servant of Christ, the queen of encouragement. She presented her entire life to the Lord as a sacrificial offering. And He did the seemingly impossible: He used a broken, pain-ridden, home-bound girl in the middle of Iowa to minister to thousands in His name.

It appeared Sara's circumstances would warrant living in anger and depression. Wouldn't those reactions to such a horrific situation be justified? Maybe, but Sara would have none of it. Instead, she chose to trust God and choose joy. God wasn't constrained by her difficulties. He didn't have limitations. And Sara knew He could overcome the real and significant obstacles in her life to use her in a great and glorious way. In the end, she trusted Him to do just that. Sara didn't understand all the reasons behind her suffering, but she trusted in the One who did right up until He took her home on September 24, 2011.

Like Sara, we have things in our lives that don't make sense. We endure pain that seems unwarranted. We face impossible situations. And like Sara, we have a choice: We can become bitter and angry, or we can trust God will redeem our circumstances. The Lord's transcendence raises Him above our problems and limitations. He has the ability to accomplish things in our lives we cannot even fathom. His love and goodness mean He will, but it may not look the way we would like it to. Sara didn't get the healing she and family and friends around the world prayed for. Instead, God chose to use her life of disease, pain, and disability to accomplish a spiritual healing in the lives of many others.

God's nature makes it possible to trust Him in our difficult situations. When we remember the greatness and otherness of our transcendent Lord, we can never claim an impossibility. Joshua didn't.

The task assigned to Joshua seemed impossible. The Israelites were to defeat Jericho, an impenetrable city with stone walls surrounding it. Yet God didn't leave Joshua to figure it out alone. He gave him the battle plans: "March around the city with all the men of war, circling the city one time. Do this for six days. . . . on the seventh day, march around the city seven times, while the priests

Sometimes I Forget

blow the rams' horns. . . . have all the troops give a mighty shout. Then the city wall will collapse" (Josh. 6:3–5). That's exactly what happened. An impossible task met the God of possibility.

God is capable of working in and through every life and every situation, no matter how unlikely it seems. So instead of giving in to anger and bitterness in our hopeless-appearing circumstances, we can rest in God's transcendence, trusting Him and choosing joy as we do.

> *Sometimes I forget, Lord, that You are* transcendent, *unbound and distinct from any other being. I forget that You are above all and beyond comprehension. I try to understand Your ways, to make sense of the workings of Your hands. But in Your transcendence, You are unlimited, capable of things far beyond my ability to know. Remind me, Lord, of Your greatness and Your otherness. Remind me that in Your infinite and perfect transcendent nature, You don't face the same limitations or problems I do. Help me remember that I can trust You to know just what I need and to accomplish the impossible in my life. You can help me defeat the giants in my life.*

TRUTH REMINDER
God knows no limits and can accomplish the impossible in my life.

29. God Is Immanent

Sometimes I forget, Lord, that You are *immanent*, nearby, caring, and active in my life. . . .

> "I will be the same until your old age, and I will bear you up when you turn gray. I have made you, and I will carry you; I will bear and rescue you." (Isa. 46:4)

> *"My life is but a weaving*
> *Between my God and me;*
> *I cannot choose the colors*
> *He worketh steadily.*
> *Sometimes He weaveth sorrow*
> *And I in foolish pride*
> *Forget He sees the upper,*
> *And I the under side.*
> *Not till the loom is silent*
> *And the shuttles cease to fly,*
> *Shall God unroll the canvas*
> *And explain the reason why.*
> *The dark threads are as needful*
> *In the Weaver's skillful hand,*
> *As the threads of gold and silver*
> *In the pattern He has planned.*
>
> FLORENCE M. ALT[33]

Sometimes I Forget

One night several years ago, I learned my son had been wounded. It was the type of hurt that cannot be seen, one that eats at the soul. My mother's heart ached to fix it, to make it all better, just like I did when he was a little boy. But I couldn't fix this pain by opening the medicine cabinet or kissing the owie. Only time and God could heal his hurting heart.

Heartbroken with my inability to help my son, I cried out to God, beseeching Him to take away all the pain. I had a plan for how He could do that and didn't waste any time explaining it to Him. (I wonder if the Lord does the God equivalent of rolling His eyes when we do that. As if we know more than He does about a situation!) Unfortunately, the only path to healing I could imagine was one that required a long time. It would be a long journey for my boy. However, the Great Physician had another idea and one far superior. The very next day He sent a godly man to speak encouragement into my son's heart, a stranger to us who made a name for himself despite his humble beginning and trial-filled upbringing. Although singing and speaking to a large audience, it was as if this man addressed his message specifically to my son who returned home uplifted and inspired in his faith. But God didn't stop there.

While my son was being ministered to, I drove an hour away to attend a Christian women's gathering. I knew this would be an enjoyable event of prayer and laughter. What I didn't expect was the powerful impact the gathering would have on my bruised heart. The entire rally centered on how Jesus never fails. We sang about His unfailing love, read Scripture pertaining to His presence and protection, listened to sermons on His mercy, and even watched a skit about His gift of salvation.

It was an inspiring day and one that assured me of God's love for me. But it wasn't until I returned home and heard about the stranger's impact on my son's life that I put it all together. At the same time the Lord was reviving a mother's spirit, He was emboldening a boy's heart forty-five miles away! That was a plan I could have never devised.

Sometimes I Forget

As we worship a supernatural God, One who is above and beyond all, so we worship a present God, One who draws near and delights in His creation. It's a great paradox of Christianity. The Lord created the world and all that's in it and remains unlimited and otherworldly, but He didn't simply create and walk away. He stays near, actively working in the world and in our lives. God is transcendent, over all and unknowable, but He is also immanent, nearby and perceivable. C. S. Lewis, in *The Problem of Pain*, put it this way: "God is both further from us, and nearer to us, than any other being."[34] He is both far and near. How awful if He remained distant and hands-off.

I didn't expect God to orchestrate the events He did that day. I knew He could but didn't necessarily consider that He would. It was a big deal to me and my son but rather small compared to so many things happening in the world. But God cares about each of us and our problems. Whether big or small by the world's standards, our concerns matter to Him. We don't need to remain alone in our suffering. The Lord is intimately involved in our lives, and He is working in the minutiae of our days to draw us to Him.

Sometimes I forget, Lord, that You are immanent, nearby, caring, and active in my life. I forget that You didn't simply create and walk away. However, sometimes in my hardest moments, it seems that way, and I feel alone and abandoned. Remind me that You remain always present and perceivable, even while You are otherworldly and unknowable, a God who is both near and far. Help me trust You as a hands-on, concerned, and loving Father. Remind me, Lord, that You are intimately involved in my life, ever working to draw me near to You.

TRUTH REMINDER
God is always close, active,
and involved in my life.

30. God Is Invisible

Sometimes I forget, Lord, that You are *invisible*, Your total essence unseen. . . .

> No one has ever seen God. (John 1:18a)

"The artist must be in his work as God is in creation, invisible and all-powerful; one must sense him everywhere but never see him."
GUSTAVE FLAUBERT[35]

I'm not sure the exact number of days I remained in darkness after my first baby passed into heaven, but each day was one too many. It blocked out everything else. I walked, talked, and breathed depression. I didn't understand why God allowed my baby to die, and I questioned His love and compassion. Until, one night, I heard from God in a dream.

As I slept, I saw a perfectly formed baby girl who looked to be around a month old. A wide-eyed beauty, she beamed at me. She was obviously being held up for me to view, but with the background faded out, I couldn't see who it was. The next instant my mind filled with words. Nothing audible, but words nonetheless.

"Here is Sarah. She's with Me and fine. Now get up and live!"

I awoke with tears trickling down my face and my baby's beautiful image seared in my mind. I hadn't told anyone her name would have been Sarah, not even my husband. Decades later, I can still see her face and "hear" the words clearly. I awoke with a renewed sense of hope. The pain of losing her hadn't left, but it

Sometimes I Forget

no longer held me in a death-like grip. I began to see life in color once again.

Being invisible, God can manifest Himself in many ways. This time He chose a dream that brought a young woman out of a deep darkness. In the pages of Exodus, we see God manifest Himself in a burning bush, a pillar of fire, and a pillar of cloud. The Psalms tell us creation declares His glory and proclaims His handiwork (Ps. 19:1). Paul writes that the Lord's invisible attributes are seen and understood through "what he has made" (Rom. 1:20). And made in His image, we reflect our Creator to others (Gen. 1:27).

Regardless of how and when God chooses to reveal Himself to us, we can count on Him being present and active in our lives. We can see the effects of His presence. We can sense Him in times of need. We can witness His hand of protection or guidance. We can see Him in others. And we can experience Him in the way we can best receive Him at the time. Far from an off-putting aspect of God, His invisibility is encouraging, giving us hope in our darkest days and in the most impossible situations.

Sometimes I forget, Lord, that You are invisible, Your total essence unseen. I forget that, although I can't see You, You're still present and active in my life. In my humanness, I miss You and what You're doing because it is so outside the realm of human possibility. But I shouldn't paint into a box an eternal, omniscient, all-powerful, invisible God. Remind me, Lord, that You can manifest Yourself in infinite ways and regularly reveal Yourself through visible, created things. Remind me to look for Your reflection in Your children. Help me see You in nature and in miraculous and not-so-miraculous happenings of daily life. Help me remember that You are always present and active in my life. I can't see You, Lord,

Sometimes I Forget

but I can see the effects of Your presence. Thank You for always revealing Yourself in the way I most need to receive You.

TRUTH REMINDER
Being invisible, God can manifest
Himself in infinite ways, meeting me
in the manner I need Him most.

31. God Is Comforting

Sometimes I forget, Lord, that You are *comforting*, coming alongside to support, counsel, and advocate. . . .

> Blessed be the God and Father of our Lord Jesus Christ, the Father of mercies and the God of all comfort. He comforts us in all our affliction, so that we may be able to comfort those who are in any kind of affliction, through the comfort we ourselves receive from God. (2 Cor. 1:3–4)

"You don't have to be alone in your hurt! Comfort is yours. Joy is an option. And it's all been made possible by your Savior. He went without comfort so you might have it. He postponed joy so you might share in it. He willingly chose isolation so you might never be alone in your hurt and sorrow."

JONI EARECKSON TADA[36]

The text message dripped with discouragement and frustration: "I don't know; he finally went to bed!! He was impossible tonight." After ascertaining that Dad was more confused than normal, I said a quick prayer and swiped another message to Mom: "I know it's hard, but he can't help not knowing what to do. But if it gets too difficult for you, we'll need to take the next step. And you don't need to [feel] guilty for that." I shared a few more words of encouragement, and Mom answered: "Thank you! It helps to vent to you!"

"I'm glad I can help." I was, and I am.

Sometimes I Forget

No, I couldn't take away the pain my mom was feeling over my dad's steady slip into dementia. I couldn't solve her problem or alleviate the burden. But I could and did give what I had: sympathy, empathy, and advice learned from experience. I could be there for her. I could comfort her through the comfort I myself had received.

Because I experienced some difficult things in my life, including being a caregiver to my young adult daughter, I understood some of what Mom was experiencing. I knew a bit about navigating the world of home care. I knew the guilt she'd have about hiring others to help with Dad's care, thinking she should be able to provide such care herself. I knew the frustration of having to repeat yourself ad nauseam. I could empathize. My ability to relate and come alongside Mom alleviated some of the loneliness she felt as her role switched from wife to caregiver. It comforted her and gave purpose to my own suffering.

In Jesus's ministry on earth, He experienced loneliness and misery at a level we'll thankfully never know. Therefore, He can relate to our own suffering. When we hurt, He consoles. When we need guidance, He counsels. When we feel alone, He comes alongside us. Our suffering is real, but so is the comfort of the Lord. And through His ministrations, He equips us to come alongside others in their need, providing a salve to both hurting hearts.

Even if we haven't experienced a similar hardship, we can still be of comfort. Often it's simply a matter of willingness to be present. Our oldest son attended college more than seven hours away. Not long into his freshman year, he surprised his siblings with a weekend visit to see our second oldest perform in a play and then returned to college on Monday. The morning of his departure, our youngest sensed my sadness at having Daniel leave again. On his way out the door to catch the school bus, Joey gave me instructions: "No crying until I get home from school, then we can cry together."

Sometimes I Forget

Joey had never experienced parenthood. He couldn't empathize with having a child grow their wings and fly from the nest. He simply sensed the depth of my sorrow, and he wanted to join me in it. To share in my misery and provide the comfort of companionship. It's a beautiful illustration of what God does for us. He comes alongside us in our suffering to strengthen and encourage, to wipe away our tears. He comes with a listening ear and a caring heart. And most encouraging of all, He comes with the promise of salvation. Jesus gave up His comfort, even His life, to secure a place for us where we will never suffer again. The Lord truly is the God of comfort.

> *Sometimes I forget, Lord, that You are* comforting, *coming alongside to support, counsel, and advocate for me, to sympathize and guide me, as I navigate this difficult road. I forget that You understand what it's like to suffer. You know how alone I feel in my pain. Help me remember, Lord, that not only can I trust You to be present, but I can trust You to be actively working in my difficult situation. Help me feel Your presence in the pain; help me experience Your peace and joy during turbulent times. Remind me, Lord, of Your promises and all that remain true, regardless of circumstances. Remind me to reach out to others with the comfort You have given me.*

TRUTH REMINDER
God is with me in my struggles, supporting, counseling, and advocating for me.

32. God Is Victorious

Sometimes I forget, Lord, that You are *victorious*, conquering sin and death. . . .

> "I have told you these things so that in me you may have peace. You will have suffering in this world. Be courageous! I have conquered the world." (John 16:33)

> *"He who sides with God cannot fail to win in every encounter; and whether the result shall be joy or sorrow, failure or success, death or life, we may, under all circumstances, join in the Apostle's shout of victory, 'Thanks be unto God which always causeth us to triumph in Christ!'"*
> HANNAH WHITALL SMITH[37]

Some of the simplest situations can produce the greatest lessons. Years ago, a couple members of my family developed a crick in their necks called wryneck. It's no fun! My daughter and a son spent five days seeing everything a bit crooked, with their heads tipped to one side. Ever an optimist, my sweet girl, who has intellectual disabilities, tries to see the hope in any situation. Periodically throughout her neck episode, she'd look at me, eyes shining, and vocalize a sound that meant "Better!?" while touching her sore muscles.

This tender gesture appeared a tentative sort of hope. Rachel wanted her neck to get better. She expected it to get better. But she wasn't quite sure if she could count on it. "I want to hope, but can I?" she seemed to ask. Sadly, many Christians walk through life this same way. We carry ourselves confidently when days run smoothly, but that assurance wanes as struggles pop up.

In our pain, we take on an air of questioning hope. Can I get through this? Will the pain ever end? Where is the joy? Will I ever be whole again? Where are God's promises now? In fact, where is God?

Yet as Christians, we never need to resort to a questioning sort of hope. Our hope is rock solid! We can count on it. An assured hope, it rests firmly on Christ Jesus. Christians hold onto a hope that began with an Infant's cry and grew through the tearing of whips and the piercing of nails. A Christian's hope is firmly anchored in the bodily resurrection of the Messiah and evidenced by an empty cross and a vacant tomb. We have a hope that does not depend on our circumstances and need not fluctuate with our feelings.

When I lost my first baby to miscarriage, I certainly didn't feel very hopeful. Nor did I have much hope following the miscarriages of four of my later children or the birth of my two children born with disabilities. Difficult circumstances shrouded the truth I knew—that victory was mine in Christ. But just because I didn't feel victorious doesn't mean it wasn't so. Our feelings don't always reflect truth.

We can know with certainty that things will get better . . . whether we've lost a loved one or are dealing with a financial crisis. We may not see it in this life, but we will have victory over our difficult situations. Jesus guaranteed it. On the cross, He defeated death itself. He conquered the enemy of our souls. He ensured all who believe in Him a resurrected life. And a resurrected life means a redeemed life, one where all things are new and there will be no more sadness or pain.

So regardless of the level of our sorrow or disappointment, we can drop the question mark surrounding our hope. Whether

Sometimes I Forget

we see it in this life or the next, for Christians, things will get better. We can stand unflinchingly on that truth. Because we stand in victory with the Victor, unshakable hope is ours.

Sometimes I forget, Lord, that You are victorious, conquering sin and death. I forget that You have also secured victory for me over sorrow and disappointment and pain. I must confess I don't always feel hopeful. I don't always see the hope. So remind me, Lord, that my feelings don't always reflect truth. Remind me that my eyes can't see the whole picture, that my finite understanding can't take in the whole picture like You do. Help me remember, Jesus, that in You, I have hope regardless of the earthly outcome of a circumstance. Remind me that You overcame for me. Thank You that I stand in victory in You.

TRUTH REMINDER
I stand in victory with the Victor, Jesus Christ whose defeat of sin and death offers hope regardless of circumstances.

33. God Is Truthful

Sometimes I forget, Lord, that You are *truthful*, never lying or acting falsely . . .

> And we know that the Son of God has come and has given us understanding, so that we may know him who is true; and we are in him who is true, in his Son Jesus Christ. He is the true God and eternal life. (1 John 5:20 ESV)

"As you go through life, don't let your feelings—real as they are—invalidate your need to let the truth of God's words guide your thinking. Remember that the path to your heart travels through your mind. Truth matters."

RANDY ALCORN[38]

I remember little about the drive home and the week following my spring break canoe trip to Arkansas my college freshman year. Sleep stole those days. Interestingly, the event itself remains clear in my mind. A group of us college students piled in a van for the long road trip from northern Iowa to "the Natural State" and a put-in point on the scenic Buffalo River. Expectations were high for a fabulous multiday float. A steady rain did little to dampen our spirits.

The second day, with temperatures in the upper 50s to low 60s, I felt safe to use my rain gear to keep the food instead of my body dry. This proved to be a near-fatal lapse in judgment. By early afternoon, our leader noticed the miserable state of many of

Sometimes I Forget

us drenched canoers and called a sandbar break to warm up and eat. For my freezing body, it was nearly too late.

Our first task was to gather wood. The forest glowed lush and inviting. Shivering violently, I wandered in that direction. Soon—as if in a bubble—I heard the crackling of a fire and my name being called. Our guide was calling me to safety. But my hypothermic condition whispered to me a lie: "Warmth lies in the trees." It compelled me forward in the wrong and potentially deadly direction. With each step farther into the woods, I experienced a deeper warmth enveloping me.

Hypothermia had hijacked my senses in the Arkansas wilds. In my skewed perspective, I tried to trade in certainty and security for what I thought looked like a better option. Warmth and safety awaited in the direction of the fire. What I felt and perceived led me the opposite way.

My distorted mindset sabotaged healthy and wise decision-making those many years ago. A phenomenon all-to-common to my life in the years since that trip. Instead of embracing all that God offers, I hold tight to my small sphere of understanding. I shy from stepping into the unknown, preferring a well-lit path. I gravitate to what I deem safe and warm. I trade in the Lord's promise of abundance for my idea of what's best. I exchange God's truth for a lie based on my perspective.

The Lord doesn't merely tell the truth, He *is* truth. His nature excludes all deceit. Friends, family, colleagues, they all may lie, but God never lies. His truth is unchanging and eternal, intricately woven into His character. Satan, however, has twisted God's truth since the garden of Eden:

> Now the serpent was the most cunning of all the wild animals that the Lord God had made. He said to the woman, "Did God really say, 'You can't eat from any tree in the garden'?"

Sometimes I Forget

> The woman said to the serpent, "We may eat the fruit from the trees in the garden. But about the fruit of the tree in the middle of the garden, God said, 'You must not eat it or touch it, or you will die.'"
>
> "No! You will certainly not die," the serpent said to the woman. "In fact, God knows that when you eat it your eyes will be opened and you will be like God, knowing good and evil." (Gen. 3:1–5)

And like Eve, we listen to the enemy's whispers of deceit: *God is withholding His goodness from you. He's lying.* In our fallen nature, we receive it and question God's truthfulness. We fall into the trap of believing peace and contentment are found on a path we fully see and understand. But the Lord confides the truth: "what is seen is temporary, but what is unseen is eternal" (2 Cor. 4:18). As our Creator, He knows we are vulnerable to deception. So as our loving Father, He provides help. He sends the Holy Spirit to guide, reveal, and convict. He gives us His Holy Word filled with truth. And He sent His Son so the relationship Adam and Eve severed with their sin could be reestablished.

God will not lie to us. He reveals only truth. So instead of following our feelings and senses, follow the One who is truth: "Then we will no longer be little children, tossed by the waves and blown around by every wind of teaching, by human cunning with cleverness in the techniques of deceit" (Eph. 4:14).

Sometimes I forget, Lord, that You are truthful, *never lying or acting falsely. I forget that Your nature excludes any deceit. So instead of embracing all You offer, I tend to hold tight to my small sphere of understanding, following my feelings and skewed perspectives. Remind me, Lord, that Your truth is intricately woven into Your character, unchanging and eternal. Help me remember to use all You provide to deflect Satan's lies and hold onto Your truth, to dig into Your Word, to come to You in prayer, to listen to the prompting of the Holy Spirit.*

TRUTH REMINDER
God will guide me in truth through the
Holy Spirit and by His holy Word.

34. God Is Lifegiving

Sometimes I forget, Lord, that You are *lifegiving*, the source and sustainer. . . .

> Jesus told him, "I am the way, the truth, and the life. No one comes to the Father except through me." (John 14:6)

> *"Of one thing I am perfectly sure: God's story never ends with 'ashes.'"*
> ELISABETH ELLIOT[39]

My lovely niece, Samantha, has no lingering effects of being born at only twenty-seven weeks' gestation. Oh, how we fought for her. The doctors and nurses worked tirelessly for nearly three months to ensure Mantha survived. Family and friends stormed the gates of heaven with our prayers, begging God to save her and her twin brother. (Sadly, Adam, his birth weight a mere 11.5 ounces, passed into Jesus's arms at just three and one-half weeks.) Once home, her parents did everything in their power to keep her healthy. But by all accounts, Samantha's life and health are miracles.

Life is that precious. Most of us will fight tooth and nail for it. The United States of America's founders included life as an unalienable right, a self-evident truth in the Declaration of Independence. We spend countless hours and dollars seeking medical attention, exercise programs, and diets to prolong our lives. Yet in our quest to save and enhance our lives, we often leave out the most important entity of life itself: the One who

Sometimes I Forget

created it. God is the Author of all life. In the beginning, on the fifth and sixth days of creation, He made creatures to fill the land, sea, and air that He had formed on days one through four. It was on that sixth day that He breathed life into man (Gen. 2:7). But that wasn't the end of His participation in our lives. He didn't just create and leave us to fend for ourselves.

As a loving Father, God chooses to do life with us. He walked in the garden of Eden with the first man and woman. He made provisions for them after they sinned and could no longer safely remain in His presence. Through the centuries, He directed, warned, led, counseled, and assured His people. We see God's hand in the lives of His people throughout the Old Testament.

Our earthly lives are amazing enough. But God didn't leave us alone to wallow in our sin forever; He promised He'd continue to be with us through the ages (Matt. 28:20). And He fulfilled that promise by sending His Son to atone for our sins, to bridge the divide that formed between His holiness and sinful man when Adam and Eve chose to disobey. He made a way for us to be in His presence again. He paved the path for His children to spend eternity with Him.

Yes, life is precious. Our earthly life is worth celebrating and fighting for. But the Lord provided something even more splendid and amazing: He gave us His Son Jesus Christ to secure a life that will never end and will never suffer again. That's a life that matters, and that's definitely a life worth fighting for.

Sometimes I forget, Lord, that You are lifegiving, the source and sustainer. I forget that You want to be in our lives, to be a loving, present Father. So I tend to run my own race, forgetting the importance of including You in it all. Remind me, Lord, of Your love for me. Help me sense Your presence and guidance. Thank You for providing the most splendid and amazing aspect of life: an

Sometimes I Forget

eternity spent in Your presence. Thank You for offering Your own Son to bridge the divide between Your Holiness and my sin, so I can once again walk with You. Help me hold all life as precious—created in Your image and set apart as sacred.

TRUTH REMINDER
God breathed life into me, will sustain me, and has promised me eternal life in Jesus Christ.

35. God Is Light

Sometimes I forget, Lord, that You are *light*, piercing through the darkness, exposing truth, and bringing hope. . . .

> Jesus spoke to them again: "I am the light of the world. Anyone who follows me will never walk in the darkness but will have the light of life." (John 8:12)

"When the dark clouds gather most, the light is the more brightly revealed to us. When the night lowers and the tempest is coming on, the Heavenly Captain is always closest to His crew."
CHARLES SPURGEON[40]

I clearly remember the day I got glasses. I was in sixth grade. None of us six kids had trouble seeing, except apparently me. We lived on a hilltop farm, and two hills over sat another farm; the Kresses were our nearest neighbors.

I stood in front of the big picture window later in the day. "Hey, did you know we can see Kress's farm from here?" I inquired of my mom. I'm not sure how long I stood there, taking my new glasses off and on. All I know is I was awed with what I could finally see.

But my enhanced vision pales in comparison to what we can see in God's light. The Lord's light illuminates the darkness of this world. But not only does He cast light, He is light in His very being, drawing us to Him and awakening us to the truth. We should be awestruck! Those who know the Lord, who walk with

Sometimes I Forget

Him, are walking with the Light of the World. The God of the universe reveals Himself to us and directs our steps. He gives sight to the blind, brightening the darkness and making us partakers of God's divine nature. By His light, He draws us to Him. He exposes any darkness in us and guides us in righteousness.

As a child, I missed some lovely sights of rolling hills and peaceful farmsteads because I was blind to distant sights. The crazy thing is, I didn't even realize what I was missing until I could finally see. Similarly, we don't know how badly we need the Light until circumstances open our eyes to the darkness that surrounds us.

To begin seeing those long-missed sights, I had to not only get the proper glasses, but I had to put them on. Buying glasses wouldn't have helped my sight if I hadn't worn them. Likewise, in order to begin experiencing the abundant life, we must walk in the light of Christ, not simply know He's there. We won't see any better by merely knowing Jesus exists. We need to welcome Him in as our Savior. And we won't be any wiser by merely possessing a Bible. God promises wisdom and understanding come through the hearing of Scripture. A closed Bible won't impart much of either.

Light is part of God's essence. Physically and spiritually, light exposes things previously hidden in the dark and it reveals our path. Those that walk in His light, know Him and can reflect His light to a hurting and lost world, which is both a privilege and a sacred calling.

Sometimes I forget, Lord, that You are light, *piercing through the darkness, exposing truth, and bringing hope. I forget that You reveal Yourself to me and desire to direct my steps; therefore, I miss out on so much of the abundance You have for me. Remind me, Lord, that You are the Light of the World. You've illuminated the path to life. Thank You for rescuing me from the darkness of evil and the sting of death. Remind me of the wisdom and understanding You provide for navigating this life through Your Word and the work of the Holy Spirit. Embolden me to take Your light to the lost and hurting.*

TRUTH REMINDER
The Lord is lighting my path with truth and providing wisdom and understanding for the journey.

36. God Is Blessed

Sometimes I forget, Lord, that You are *blessed*, delighting fully in Yourself and in all that reflects You. . . .

> Blessed is the God and Father of our Lord Jesus Christ, who has blessed us with every spiritual blessing in the heavens in Christ. (Eph. 1:3)

"God is blessed essentially, primarily, originally, of himself such, and not by the help of any other thing."
EDWARD LEIGH[41]

Smiling faces light up the stadium. Genuine I'm-having-the-time-of-my-life smiles, not fake I'll-smile-because-I-should kind. Nearly every participant displays such a grin. Laughter and squeals of delight intermix with "Good job!" "Nice try!" and "You can do it!"

My daughter, Rachel, kicks the ball. Even before it stops, she raises her hands in victory, eyes sparkling, laughter ringing through the air! The ball falls way short of the goal. Rachel celebrates anyway. Moving to the next event, she is too busy waving to those around her to listen to the instructions. But, the ball's there. The kick . . . short. Still, she signals . . . victory!

My daughter moves from one ball to the next during this Special Olympics soccer event. She cheers every kick, even when the ball moves a mere foot. Never letting go of her smile, she invites the audience to celebrate with her. Rachel delights in her abilities and in those who are there to celebrate with her.

Sometimes I Forget

I look around the stadium and see my daughter's joy repeated in nearly every athlete. This is no normal sporting event where winning becomes the only measure of success and the sole reason for satisfaction and happiness. The participants in the stadium this day are all impaired intellectually, but they have little impairment in their ability to display blessedness. In fact, they represent God well in this aspect of His character.

God is blessed in and of Himself. His self-existence and self-sufficiency show He needs nothing else to be complete. He is fulfilled in and of Himself and, therefore, fully enjoys Himself. God's blessedness flows from His identity, the perfection of all His attributes. He never waits for something to improve His divine life; He exists perfectly blessed.

God didn't create us because He has a need for us. He created us out of His grace and love. That should lead us to worship in acknowledgment and gratitude for all He blesses us with—the breath of life and all we possess. No, God doesn't need our happiness, but He is pleased when we imitate His blessedness by enjoying the things He gives us and appreciating and even celebrating who He made us to be. Rachel and her fellow Special Olympics athletes do this better than most of us. They find delight in who they are and what they can do. They reflect His glory well in their ability to love well, enjoy the smaller/lesser things in life, and give grace. They imitate God's blessedness in the way they celebrate their own blessedness.

God created each of us uniquely to reflect Him. So instead of disparaging what we don't have and who we aren't, let's celebrate what we possess and the characteristics God created us with. That's when we'll begin to better see the true glory and awesomeness of God. Then we'll better display His blessedness to the world. Know the Blessed and live blessed.

Sometimes I Forget

Sometimes I forget, Lord, that You are blessed, *delighting fully in Yourself and in all that reflects You. I forget that You delight in blessing us from Your blessedness. I feel slighted, missing the gifts You impart to me. Remind me, Lord, of how blessed I am. Remind me that it is pleasing to You when I embrace the abilities and characteristics You've endowed me with. Guide me to celebrate the gifts I have, rather than lamenting the ones I don't. Help me to be happy in who I am and what I've received from You. But most of all, help me to delight in You, the source of all my good and pleasing qualities and possessions, exalting You instead of dwelling on what I lack.*

TRUTH REMINDER
The Lord delights in blessing me and is glorified and exalted when I celebrate who He made me to be and appreciate all He gives me.

37. God Is Perfect

Sometimes I forget, Lord, that You are *perfect*, flawless and lacking nothing. . . .

> "Be perfect, therefore, as your heavenly Father is perfect." (Matt. 5:48)

"I am careful not to confuse excellence with perfection. Excellence I can reach for; perfection is God's business."
MICHAEL J. FOX[42]

My daughter's whimper stopped me mid-sentence. Racing back to the bathroom, I left my husband to clean up the vomit from Rachel's bed and floor. Lifting her wet, shivering body to standing in the bathtub, I succeeded in adjusting the water temp before it scalded her. Fighting back tears, I gently lowered my vomit-covered twenty-four-year-old into the now-warm water, silently chastising myself while outwardly calming her fears.

I pride myself on having things together, being capable and dependable. This night shredded that idea. With Rachel's bedroom on the north side of the house and ours on the south, I hadn't heard her cry for help when she first got sick. She'd likely been laying in her vomit for a couple hours. Our son alerted us to her needs. Then in my hurry to get her cleaned up, comforted, and back to bed, I nearly burned the poor girl. Could I be any more of a failure as a parent?

Months later, I still find it difficult to write about this situation, partly because it really makes me sound like an awful parent/

caregiver. I'm also hesitant to share it because it highlights my imperfections, those areas in my life I'd like to keep hidden. I tend to strive for perfection in all areas of my life. But expecting that I can achieve such a thing is foolish and prideful. Projecting a perfect persona may make me look better, but it makes other Christians feel like they're lacking.

It's important to know we aren't alone in our shortcomings and sins. And it's critical we don't equate imperfection with faithlessness. If that were the case, not one human being (apart from the incarnate Jesus) would be considered to have faith. Consider the "Heroes of the Faith" found in Hebrews 11: Sarah laughed at God; Abraham tried to take things under his own control; Moses repeatedly questioned God and begged off of his assignment; King David committed adultery and had a man killed to cover it up. Not one of these individuals would have been held up as a standard of faith based on their conduct. They were approved by faith and faith alone. God approves us, too, imperfections and all, when we believe in Jesus Christ as our Lord and Savior, and that's an act of faith made possible through His grace, not our works.

If we expect and believe we can lead perfect lives, we'll have no room in our lives for our perfect God—a God who perfectly deals with His flawed children. His completeness gives us hope in our imperfections. The Lord's perfect love supplies hope for eternity. His perfect mercy offers forgiveness for our sins. His perfect grace provides possibility in the brokenness of our humanity. His perfect justice gives us the perfect Savior.

It's in the perfection of God that we find peace in this life of imperfection. His moral completeness assures us of His faithfulness and allows us to trust the flawlessness of His redemption plan for us. It gives us reason to worship and praise the glorious Savior. And it promises us sanctification as we walk forward in grace.

Sometimes I Forget

Sometimes I forget, Lord, that You are perfect, flawless and lacking nothing. I forget that, in Your perfect nature, You know my limitations and provide for them. In foolishness and pride, I set myself up for failure. Instead of surrendering to Your perfect work, I try to achieve it myself and despair when I cannot. Remind me of Your perfect love that supplies hope for eternity, Your perfect mercy that offers forgiveness for my sins, Your perfect grace that provides possibility in the brokenness of my humanity, and Your perfect faithfulness that allows me to trust the flawlessness of Your redemption plan for me. It's in Your moral completeness that I find peace in this life of imperfection. Thank You, Lord.

TRUTH REMINDER
In His flawless nature, God provides for
all I lack in my imperfection.

38. God Is Eternal

Sometimes I forget, Lord, that You are *eternal*, You have always existed, and You always will. . . .

> Before the mountains were born,
> before you gave birth to the earth and the world,
> from eternity to eternity, you are God.
> (Ps. 90:2)

"As well might a gnat seek to drink in the ocean, as a finite creature to comprehend the Eternal God. A God whom we could understand would be no God. If we could grasp him he could not be infinite: if we could understand him, then were he not divine."

CHARLES SPURGEON[43]

Dishes left soaking, I stare off into the brooding sky, forcing my thoughts to a distant time. A time that holds many concerns and too-few assurances. With clenched jaw, I will myself to stay in that place a little longer, pondering the future of our adult daughter, Rachel, who has special needs. Questions flit in and out of my mind like hummingbirds grabbing sips of nectar.

When will we know it's time to find a home for her? How will I possibly be able to let strangers care for her 24/7? How can we be sure her needs are being met? How will they know what she really likes? Do we have to place her in another home? Is there another way? Who's going to protect her from the evil that waits to pounce?

Sometimes I Forget

A stray tear slips out. *Lord, it's too much.* Life is too much. With its unexpected twists and turns. Its tears and heartaches. And the unknowns. The dreaded unknowns! Time marches on, relentless. It burns up the minutes we've set aside for projects and relationships. The candle burns out while we grasp for simply another flicker. That's my concern: time running out for me but continuing for my daughter. The unknown future. How do I prepare . . . myself and her?

Yet time is the Lord's as is everything else. He created it. He rules it. And one day, when we're in heaven, time won't have a hold on us. As I ponder my daughter's future, I cling to the eternality of God. He has always been and always will be. Therefore, I can trust He'll be there for Rachel when I no longer can be. And in His good and loving nature, He'll take care of her.

The past can grip us with its memories of things to hide from and even ones to cling to. The present can overwhelm us with its trials and frustrations. But the future can paralyze us with its unwelcome possibilities. Yet, comfort and peace lie in the truth that God is the Lord of all time—past, present, and future. He is sovereign across all time and before time. And He exercises His perfect will for all of eternity.

God's will does not end when our earthly life ends. His faithfulness remains as it has been. Since He holds our lives in His infinitely loving and gracious hands, we can let go of our hold on our future concerns. The Lord remains supreme for all of eternity. His perfect will is and always will be exercised right on time. That gives us all hope in whatever may lie ahead in this life, for us and for those we love, and the promise of being with Him in the next.

Sometimes I forget, Lord, that You are eternal, You have always existed, and You always will. I forget that You are timeless, being outside the realm of anything I can understand. Not only that, but You created time. It is in Your hand to use as You see fit. Still, I get

Sometimes I Forget

impatient and question why You don't act sooner or wait longer. I become concerned about what the future holds for me and for those I love. Remind me, Lord, of Your sovereignty over time and of Your eternal love and faithfulness. Help me remember that You remain supreme for all of eternity and that Your perfect will is and always will be exercised right on time. Forgive me for doubting You. Help me rest in Your complete and everlasting nature until I dwell in my eternal home with You.

TRUTH REMINDER
God has always existed and always will, so His timing in my life and in the lives of those I love is perfect.

39. God Is Majestic

Sometimes I forget, Lord, that You are *majestic*, of splendid character and grandeur. . . .

> LORD, our Lord,
> how magnificent is your
> name throughout the earth!
> You have covered the heavens with your
> majesty. (Ps. 8:1)

> *"You might as well not be alive if
> you're not in awe of God."*
> ALBERT EINSTEIN[44]

After hours of trekking through deep woods and up steep hillsides, I came to the junction I sought. Taking a left, I wove my way along a faint trail through deep brush for another mile. I began to question my sense of direction and my sanity when, finally, the trail dumped me out at the edge of the world. I stood on a rocky point that jutted out into space. Below me in three directions sat a carpet of dark treetops, the sky stretching endlessly above it. I breathed in the view for a few minutes before scrambling back to the nearest campsite. This sanctuary was all mine for the moment, and I wanted to stake my claim.

With daylight waning, I set up camp and quickly prepared a warm meal to take out to the rocky point. I had heard magic happened on this rock in the bookends of the day and was determined not to miss a minute of it. Night fell swiftly, cloaking

Sometimes I Forget

me in darkness and solitude. With only the stars as distractions, I sensed God's presence in a way I rarely do. But I knew this was only the beginning. Much more awaited in the predawn hours, so I retreated to my tent for some rest.

While the world slept, an early-morning alarm sent me dressing and out of my tent. A deep fog had settled in overnight, so I painstakingly crept to the spot on the rock I claimed as mine. Enveloped in the fog, the isolation was complete, but not for too long. I sensed the sun before I saw it, inching its way above the horizon. Then with a burst that startled me, it topped the trees. I stopped mid-bite of my granola bar, frozen by a sight so otherworldly it took my breath away. God's glory and greatness, His brilliance, was on display. Below me flowed a sea of fog, covering the treetops as far as I could see. It's fingers stretching and contracting as the sun began to burn it back. I sat in awe for hours watching God's handiwork and communing with Him until the sun finally chased away the final vestiges of mist.

I feel God's grandeur best in places like the expansive Boundary Waters in northern Minnesota or the dense woods and high cliffs of the Red River Gorge in Kentucky, where the magnificence of God is written in the vastness and closeness of the sky. In these isolated, wild places where the heavens kiss the earth, God's splendor moves from something I know of to something that captures my heart.

Nature's magnificence speaks to a greatness we cannot comprehend. It speaks to the majesty of the Creator and Sustainer of the universe. It reveals the magnitude of the One who holds us in His hands, reminding us that He is God, and we are not.

We all need these moments. Time away from our comfortable, predictable, daily lives to encounter our great God. In a place and posture of solitude we can welcome in the fullness of His splendor. When we stop and consider His wonders, the greatness and majesty of His character, we remember He's big enough

Sometimes I Forget

to help us through our most troubling days. Such evidence of His grandeur draws us into His presence and compels our hearts to a posture of surrender and worship—exactly where they should be.

Sometimes I forget, Lord, that You are majestic, of splendid character and grandeur. I forget that You possess unequaled might and beauty. Actually, I forget You, Lord, and get lost in my daily concerns. Open my eyes to see You in the happenings and beings of creation. Let morning sunrises and gentle winds remind me of Your presence. Let booming thunderstorms and crashing surfs wake me to an awareness of Your greatness and brilliance. Let soaring mountaintops and vast skyscapes declare Your glory. Let my heart sing with continuous worship and praise as I behold You in all Your splendor. May Your creation remind me that You are big enough to defeat all of my giants. Stir in me reverence and awe for Your majesty.

TRUTH REMINDER
God is majestic: unfailingly present, matchless in might and beauty, and faithful to help me through my most troubling days.

40. God Is Peaceful

Sometimes I forget, Lord, that You are *peaceful*, tranquil and quiet of spirit. . . .

> "Peace I leave with you. My peace I give to you. I do not give to you as the world gives. Don't let your heart be troubled or fearful." (John 14:27)

> *"Hear me very carefully on this point. Nobody can take your peace from you. If you have lost your peace, you have lost it for one main reason—you have surrendered it."*
> CHARLES F. STANLEY[45]

There he lay, propped on his side. The little plastic penguin seemed to mock the weight of my sadness. Less than an hour earlier my usually happy daughter had thrown this favorite little toy in anger (or was it frustration?), the beginning of a downward spiral in her demeanor that ended with her in bed and me feeling defeated.

For weeks we struggled to identify the cause of Rachel's newly manifested mood swings. Her limited ability to express herself makes diagnosis difficult. Medical, hormonal, behavioral, or a combination—we often don't know. She was hurting in some way, and my heart ached for her. I spent sleepless hours searching for the cause. I scoured various resources for a solution. I longed for peace for my precious girl as well as for me and my husband.

During life's struggles, it can be difficult to find rest and tranquility. We play scenarios over in our minds, trying to discover a solution or a way to simply keep moving. We ask the why and

Sometimes I Forget

what if questions. We beg God for answers or maybe simply for relief from the onslaught of grief and frustration. We wonder how we can keep our aching hearts from breaking into a million tiny pieces. In our pain, it seems impossible. But there's hope. With God, there's always hope.

That next morning, the one after Mr. Penguin lost his favored position, I opened my Bible and reread the perfect reminder:

> "Though the mountains move
> and the hills shake,
> my love will not be removed from you
> and my covenant of peace will not be shaken,"
> says your compassionate LORD. (Isa. 54:10)

This beautiful Scripture passage assures us that we can have peace no matter what trials come our way. And it's ours forever. God's precious peace borne on a life raft of His love is mine and yours to keep. The waves pound it, the gale-force winds attempt to swamp it, yet His love-raft holds, His peace is never washed overboard. We can count on the deliverance of that peace because we can count on the One who brings it. The Lord doesn't change. He remains the same faithful, gracious, victorious God from eternity to eternity!

Although originally penned for the Israelites, the beautiful words from the prophet Isaiah hold true for us as well. So, although its often hard to grasp, you don't have to wonder if there's the possibility of finding peace in the middle of the fiercest storm. The answer is yes. God promises it, and because He is peace in His very being, we can trust His promise.

Oh, the storms may at times be fierce, the mountains may indeed seem to be crumbling around us, but we can stand on the character of God. And God's unmovable love promises us unshakable peace.

Sometimes I Forget

During the most awful diagnoses, during the most painful losses, we have a life raft to grab. And it will do more than keep us afloat. The immutable, infinite, steadfast God of light and life delivers a peace we never thought possible, even when being buffeted by impossible winds. All we have to do is turn to Him and receive it (Phil. 4:6–7). What are you waiting for?

Sometimes I forget, Lord, that You are peaceful, tranquil and quiet of spirit. I forget that You are not flustered by my circumstances and that I don't have to be. I fix my eyes on my situation instead of on You, and get anxious and worried. Remind me, Lord, that I am stamped with Your image, so I, too, have access to Your peace. Help me remember to turn to You in my struggles, to open my heart to the salve of Your grace, and to trust that it will always be there for me. Regardless of my circumstances, calm my spirit, give me a quietness and trust that transcends all understanding.

TRUTH REMINDER
God offers me tranquility and quietness in my spirit even when life is chaotic and confusing.

41. God Is Steadfast

Sometimes I forget, Lord, that You are *steadfast*, loyal and dependable. . . .

> We have this as a sure and steadfast anchor of the soul, a hope that enters into the inner place behind the curtain. (Heb. 6:19 ESV)

"God will not be absent when His people are on trial; he will stand in court as their advocate, to plead on their behalf."
CHARLES H. SPURGEON[46]

"I wish Rachel was autistic!"

Between sobs, the sentiment burst out, dripping with self-condemnation. I cringed in horror at what I had just uttered about my sweet daughter. But the words were finally out, released from a prison where they had festered for far too long. Now they hung out for all to hear . . . and judge.

I wanted an answer. So, in my distraught mind, autism, as terribly difficult a diagnosis as it is, would be better than nothing. Surely answers would salve the pain and bring a little hope. The counselor waited, knowing more would come now that the dam had burst. And I didn't disappoint.

This was a lifetime ago. My world was imploding. I had experienced five miscarriages over a ten-year period. We had three rambunctious boys, ages eight, six, and one, who brought stresses of their own. We had a daughter who, at the age of four couldn't talk, had just learned to walk, and experienced significant delays in all areas of development. We had no reason for Rachel's delays and no road map for her future. And I was trying to handle it all on my own strength.

God was out there, I knew, but He felt distant. Mired in fear, I couldn't comprehend how Rachel's disabilities could be okay. I desperately needed a reason to hope. But I was placing my hope in man—in doctors and therapists—and in my own strength and that of my husband. Instead of trusting God with my difficult circumstances, I foolishly anchored my hope in something that would never hold. After walking with the Lord for decades and through much hardship, I should have known I could depend on Him. But I didn't.

When we feel unmoored and insecure, it's our problem, not God's. He never wavers in His dedication and faithfulness to us. From the beginning, when the Lord breathed life into our lungs and said, "It was very good" (Gen. 1:31), He has shown unswerving loyalty to us. Even though we turn away from Him to other idols, He remains firm in His love and always will. How do we know? There's plenty of evidence in the Scriptures.

God's true nature rings through the Old Testament. Through the centuries, God has remained faithful to the Israelites despite their continual infidelity (Exodus and others). We see His steadfastness to David despite the king's grievous sins (1 Samuel; 2 Samuel; 1 Kings 1). He never wavered in His commitment to Abraham and Sarah, despite Sarah's disbelief and Abraham's self-reliance (Gen. 12–25).

And His steadfast nature continues to be on display throughout the New Testament: Saul (later Paul) claimed to be the greatest of sinners as one who personally murdered Christians before he converted (1 Tim. 1:15), yet God elevated him to one of the most prolific and well-known apostles. Peter abandoned and disowned Jesus, but the Lord reinstated him as a shepherd for

Sometimes I Forget

His lost sheep (John 18, 21). The law demanded the adulteress be stoned, yet Jesus assured her of His love and mercy (John 8:1–11).

Our circumstances sometimes overwhelm us and blind us to the loyalty and trustworthiness of our God. We grow weary and turn to things other than Him for our security. The Holy Spirit will help us grow increasingly steadfast as we walk with Him. But even when our faith becomes shaky, God stands steadfast in His love for us. Despite our infidelity, the Lord remains completely and utterly dependable . . . for eternity.

> *Sometimes I forget, Lord, that You are* steadfast, *loyal and dependable. I forget that You remain faithful despite our unfaithfulness. Therefore, when trials come, I doubt and turn to other things for security. Remind me, Lord, of Your steadfast love. Remind me that You will not abandon nor forsake me. You promise to be with me and to strengthen and guide me through all life's struggles. No matter how bad things appear to be, help me learn to trust You, to become increasingly steadfast and unmovable in my faith. Thank You for being completely and utterly dependable forever and ever.*

TRUTH REMINDER
The Lord remains steadfast, strengthening and guiding me through this life and into eternity.

42. God Is Incomprehensible

Sometimes I forget, Lord, that You are *incomprehensible*, mysterious and beyond understanding. . . .

> "The LORD who made the earth, the LORD who forms it to establish it, the LORD is his name, says this: Call to me and I will answer you and tell you great and incomprehensible things you do not know." (Jer. 33:2–3)

"As well might a gnat seek to drink in the ocean, as a finite creature to comprehend the Eternal God."

CHARLES H. SPURGEON[47]

I have prayed for many things in my life. I prayed for the lives of my unborn children— that I could hold each one. I prayed for my sweet daughter—that she would think like others her age. I prayed for easy living—that I'd have many things to enjoy and more to give away. None of my prayers included pain. God did hear, and He did answer. But it wasn't the answer I wanted. The Lord didn't keep pain at bay; however, He did provide me with His presence and grace through it all—much greater gifts than I could have imagined.

It's been a hard journey, for sure. One filled with deep grief, confusion, and anger. But it's also held great joy and promise. The Lord poured out blessings I never knew I needed and never would have thought to ask for. I prayed for the good gift of my children to hold, love, and nurture. A worthy request. But in

Sometimes I Forget

His sovereignty and grace, He bestowed on me different gifts, ones that would stretch me and grow me in ways I never knew I needed.

God grew in me a faith that, while it still bends some, it does not break. He drew me nearer to Him. He gave me empathy and compassion for women who struggle to have babies. He filled our home with the joy of four children. He strengthened me to provide long-term for our daughter. He opened the door for me to share His love and grace with others in a writing ministry. He's given me opportunities to pour encouragement into the lives of other parents who are raising children with disabilities. He's taught me to place my security in Him.

We usually ask God to grant the desires of our hearts. But our hearts aren't always (perhaps rarely) in tune with God's will—with His best for us. You see, we ask for the possible, and God delivers the impossible. We beg for the logical, and He provides the supernatural. God doesn't give as we expect. It sometimes seems He's taking, but He's actually giving far more and in a profoundly different way than what makes sense to us, in part, because our minds cannot fully comprehend our eternal, glorious, holy, self-sufficient, loving God. In His incomprehensible nature, His actions don't always appear loving or just or gracious to us. We grossly underestimate what the Lord can do in our lives. I know I did.

> *Sometimes I forget, Lord, that You are incomprehensible, mysterious and beyond understanding. I forget that the desires of my heart don't always align with what You know to be best in my life. Forgive me, Lord, when I doubt and grow angry. Salve the pain when You answer my good prayers differently than I'd like. Remind me of Your great love for me, a love that cost Jesus everything and gave me the fullness of life. Remind me that I can't*

possibly understand fully what You do, but I can trust in Your perfect will. You know all, Lord. Help me rest in Your mysterious and unfathomable nature, even when it makes no sense to me.

TRUTH REMINDER

God's ways are often mysterious, but in His perfect will He always provides for my best.

43. God Is Impassible

Sometimes I forget, Lord, that You are *impassible*, self-controlled and purposeful in all Your emotions. . . .

> "Furthermore, the Eternal One of Israel does not lie or change his mind, for he is not man who changes his mind." (1 Sam. 15:29)

"His [God's] emotions befit a divine being who is Spirit, immortal, incorrupt and so on. So he never lets rage nor sadness overcome him. Whatever God feels, he does so as God and not as we are. And such emotions (or whatever we should call them) express via God's simple, immutable nature."

WYATT GRAHAM[48]

Red-faced, I clenched my teeth while furiously clicking from one menu item to another on my computer screen, determined to correct the problem. Only the second original post on my new blog site, and its link was broken. I had spent most of the afternoon trying to correct it. Frustration outweighed reason at this point.

"Mom, is it that important?" ventured my college son, recently home on break.

Important. . . . Important! Only everyone will be judging my abilities as an encourager based on having this post up. Followers may become frustrated and leave. That will reduce my platform and then no agents or publishers will look at my work. And I've wasted so much time and money attending writers' conferences and promoting my work for nothing. . . .

Sometimes I Forget

That's the tirade I wanted to say. Instead, I hissed an emphatic, "Yes, it is!" as I continued to pound out possible solutions. Hot tears spilled down my cheeks as I mumbled to myself about the unfairness of the situation and how I was so ill-equipped for this endeavor and how my much more tech-savvy son was doing his own thing instead of helping me.

Eventually, a fix presented itself. The emotionally charged situation waned. My ever-astute boy began again: "Mom, you understand you were crying over a compu—" *Yes, son, a computer. But it was important. . . .*

I wish I could say this was a rare scene for me—losing control over "important," but not that important, matters. Sadly, it is not. I'm afraid many of us react based on our feelings far too often. Some of us let our emotions dictate what we believe and how we act most of the time. All of us are emotionally swayed in our lives on some level. And sometimes it changes us into someone we don't know and don't want to be, leaving us red-faced with regret.

Thankfully, God never responds to us or our world in the way our emotions sway us. He loves us, for sure, and suffered for us in Christ. But can you imagine if the Lord reacted as our behaviors warrant? How fearful it would be to wonder if our next mean word or careless act might set off the Almighty! God's impassivity assures us that we can trust His promises. He will follow through as He promised in perfect agreement with His nature. Nothing we do will take away His love. Nothing we do will affect His righteousness and the free gift of grace He's given us through Jesus Christ.

The Lord acts in agreement with His self-sufficient, self-existent, perfect, holy, and unchanging character. When I say, "My confidence is the Lord," I can be assured because His promises will stand (see Jer. 17:7–8). He is self-controlled. Emotions won't overcome Him. God isn't weakened by sorrow or pain.

Sometimes I Forget

He does express grief and love, but it's in accordance with His patience, holiness, and perfect plan.

I'm afraid I'll continue to have red-faced moments of regret. Occasionally I will let something get under my skin and bring my emotions to the surface (or cause them to spill over). I'm certain I'm not alone in that. Hopefully, it happens less often the longer we walk with the Lord. But when it does, we can take comfort in God's impassive nature. When we react in anger, He continues in love. When we cry out in bitterness, He persists in mercy. When we give up in defeat, He remains victorious. The character of God transcends emotions. He is totally self-controlled, always acting on purpose. And that assures us hope remains.

Sometimes I forget, Lord, that You are impassible, *self-controlled and purposeful in all Your emotions. I sometimes forget that I can always count on Your steadfast love and new mercies. However, Your nature assures me that I can trust in You. Remind me that You don't act rashly. You aren't prone to mood swings or weakened by sorrow or pain. Assure me that my confidence in Your goodness and grace and righteousness is warranted. Although You love and grieve, You do so on purpose. Help me remember that You are never overcome by feelings as I am. You always act in accordance with Your perfect nature. So although I react impulsively and inappropriately at times, You remain my hope.*

TRUTH REMINDER
God always responds to me and to the world in a way that is consistent with His loving, just, and holy nature.

44. God Is Forgiving

Sometimes I forget, Lord, that You are *forgiving*, dismissing and forgetting my sins. . . .

> For you, Lord, are kind and ready to forgive,
> abounding in faithful love to all who call on you.
> (Ps. 86:5)

> *"I have seen Christians in Communist prisons with fifty pounds of chains on their feet, tortured with red-hot iron pokers, in whose throats spoonfuls of salt had been forced, being kept afterward without water, starving, whipped, suffering from cold—and praying with fervor for the Communists. This is humanly inexplicable! It is the love of Christ, which was poured out in our hearts."*
> RICHARD WURMBRAND[49]

Every time I thought about her and what she had done to me, anger bubbled up. She had no right to say the things she said and treat me the way she did. Although I had been nice to her, she had turned around and threw it back in my face. I deserved better. I knew I should forgive her, but honestly, I didn't want to.

So when I read about Richard Wurmbrand, a Christian pastor in Romania imprisoned and tortured under the Communist regime for fourteen years, I recoiled at the depth of my pride and self-centeredness. This man suffered unimaginable horrors, yet he forgave his torturers. I struggle to comprehend that. But he's not alone. Through the centuries countless martyrs have been

Sometimes I Forget

systemically tortured and killed, forgiving their persecutors as they died. That goes against all human logic. But not divine love.

Pastor Wurmbrand explains the unexplainable this way: ". . . Christ loves them. So does every person who has the mind of Christ."[50]

While hanging on the cross, Jesus asked His Father to forgive the very people who nailed Him there (Luke 23:34). Imagine! Only out of great love can such a thing be done. And the Lord has great love. A love that He pours out on us. A love that can drive us to forgive as He has forgiven. A love that led Pastor Wurmbrand and many other martyrs to release the injustices that had been done to them.

Pastor Wurmbrand emulated Jesus in forgiving his perpetrators while they still sinned against him. While we continue to sin, Jesus continues to dismiss the charges against us. He releases us from God's just penalty while we're still guilty. That's what makes the Lord's forgiveness so incredible! It's given freely without ever being deserved.

Jesus calls us to forgiveness too, but we won't do it perfectly. We will often hold tight to our grievances, refusing to offer forgiveness until either our offender asks for it or, in our mind, deserves it. The apostle Paul put it this way: "For I do not understand what I am doing, because I do not practice what I want to do, but I do what I hate" (Rom. 7:15). When we do that, we belittle the gift God freely gives to every Christian.

But when we love more like Christ, we forgive more like Him. Love and forgiveness go hand in hand. As we steep ourselves in the love of the Lord, we'll begin to forgive more genuinely and more quickly.

I eventually forgave the lady who offended me. Pastor Wurmbrand forgave those who exacted horrific suffering on him. Neither of us did it perfectly like Christ does us. But out of His

Sometimes I Forget

endless love and forgiveness, we can forgive too. It's a gift for us to extend to those who don't deserve it, exactly how we receive it.

Sometimes I forget, Lord, that You are forgiving, dismissing and forgetting my sins. I sometimes forget that out of Your great love for me, You chose to extend great mercy to me. When I miss the incredible gift of Your forgiveness, I tend to hold tight to grievances I have with others. Remind me that, in Christ, You saved me from the curse of sin. Remind me that You released me from all of Your just penalties, even dismissing the charges against me, a gift none of us deserves. And help me, Lord, extend that same forgiveness to my offenders.

TRUTH REMINDER
In Christ, God forgives me of all my sins and calls me to forgive others who sin against me.

45. God Is Healing

Sometimes I forget, Lord, that You are *healing*, restoring and making all whole. . . .

> But he was pierced because of our rebellion,
> crushed because of our iniquities;
> punishment for our peace was on him,
> and we are healed by his wounds. (Isa. 53:5)

"God can heal wounds that no medicine ever can."
ANONYMOUS[51]

How many times have I looked at my daughter and wondered why God hasn't offered His healing to her? He has the power. I know that. He is the Great Physician.

God could heal her through water, like at the pool of Bethesda (John 5:1–14). He could heal her by speaking words, like He did for the centurion's servant (Matt. 8:5–13). He could heal her by smearing her with mud (John 9:1–12), by touching her with His nail-scarred hands (Mark 5:37–42), or by simply delivering the healing through the gifts of others. But for reasons only He knows, God hasn't chosen to do any of those.

Maybe you're also wondering why the Lord hasn't healed your loved one. *Hasn't He seen the suffering? Doesn't He care?* Once they start, the questions keep coming. Why does God heal some and not others? Isn't it good and right to heal all sick babies, disabled children, or dying mothers? What is He waiting for?

Sometimes I Forget

Good questions. And the answer to each of them is: We don't fully know.

Perhaps God hasn't physically healed because He cares more about the spiritual healing. Perhaps He's using the situation to shape, mold, and guide us to a more intimate relationship with Him. Perhaps it's because He loves us so deeply that He can't stand to watch us live self-absorbed lives, pursuing an elusive joy in the trappings of this fallen world. Maybe God doesn't provide the healing because He knows a thorn in our side on earth is better than an eternity in hell. Maybe God allows the pain and suffering we experience in this world because He loves us too much not to.

There are times, though, when God does choose to heal in this lifetime. And it's not easy to see others healed while you or a loved one remains infirm. That's when a seed of bitterness can take root. Let's not allow that to happen! We can ask the Holy Spirit for help. And we can preach truth to ourselves: the truth that the Lord is trustworthy, that He loves all of us, and that He has a good plan. We don't need to know the plan to believe in it, because we serve One who is perfect and holy.

No, my daughter has not yet received healing on earth. Neither has my son nor many other faithful followers of Christ. The reason why remains a mystery. But as long as we know they are sheltered under the divine hand of the Master, we can have peace, trusting that one day the story will be different.

> *Sometimes I forget, Lord, that You are healing, restoring and making all whole. I forget that, as the Great Physician, You work to mend mind, body, and soul. All around me I see disability, injury, sickness, sin, mental illness, and death and become discouraged. Yet You are acting purposely. Remind me of Your great understanding, infinite knowledge, and perfect timing. Remind me*

Sometimes I Forget

of Your everlasting love, compassion, and justice. Remind me that You care. And help me remember, Lord, that healing doesn't always mean a strong and healthy physical body and it doesn't always happen in this lifetime. You promise Your abundant grace will carry me through when I don't see the hand of healing. Thank You, though, that as Your child, I am ultimately healed from all sin and physical ailments once and for all in heaven.

TRUTH REMINDER
God doesn't always heal in the manner or timing that I desire, but He will make all whole and complete in heaven.

46. God Is Spirit

Sometimes I forget, Lord, that You are *spirit*, immaterial and existing outside the physical realm. . . .

> "God is spirit, and those who worship him must worship in Spirit and in truth." (John 4:24)

> *". . . as a pure perfect Spirit . . . We cannot have an adequate or suitable conception of God: He dwells in inaccessible light; inaccessible to the acuteness of our fancy, as well as the weakness of our sense."*
> STEPHEN CHARNOCK[52]

I cracked the door open and stepped inside. Soft light and quiet stillness met me. Not wanting to disturb the few individuals present, I eased the door closed and slipped into a padded pew. I settled my Bible in my lap and lost myself in prayer while I waited for news about my son's heart ablation. As I sat in the hush of the prayer chapel, a doctor sought to ablate an extra electrical pathway in Zachary's heart (apparently, one is enough).

The procedure is quite successful with low risk, but the worst-case scenario remained. So I sought out a quiet place to lay my concerns before God. I prayed for guidance for the physicians' hands, a great physical outcome, and peace and comfort for all of us. I was doing what Scripture counsels: "Don't worry about anything, but in everything, through prayer and petition with thanksgiving, present your requests to God" (Phil. 4:6).

Sometimes I Forget

The Lord answered. As I sat in that little hospital chapel communing with Him, an image came to my mind. A divine hand held the catheter, threading it through my boy's heart. The impression lasted only a second, but in that instant, I knew all was well. The doctor didn't have final say over the outcome of Zach's ablation; my son rested in the hands of the Great Physician.

God doesn't always reveal Himself in such a profound and obvious way. Often His presence remains unseen. But His works give evidence of His nearness. Being immaterial, the Lord isn't constrained by space. He can be in Zach's body; He was then and remains so. In fact, the third person of the Trinity resides in each of us Christians. And God isn't limited to one place at a time. He can be (and was) both guiding the doctor and visiting me. It gives me chills as I type such deep mysteries!

The Lord certainly works in our lives in mysterious and miraculous ways. His spiritual nature is at once confounding and comforting. Confounding in a "way out of our league" sort of way. Comforting in knowing He can do vastly more than we understand or even imagine (Eph. 3:20). Our God cannot be perceived by our bodily senses unless He chooses to reveal Himself in that way. Instead, He "speaks" to us in the spirit of our hearts. Regardless, we can be assured that wherever we go, God abides with us still. What peace such a truth brings.

Sometimes I forget, Lord, that You are spirit, *immaterial and existing outside the physical realm. I forget that, as a spiritual being, You are not limited to any specific space. You have no form or substance, and so I can become frustrated in my attempt to know and understand You. Yet You manifest Yourself in many ways in and through Your creation. Remind me, Lord, that wherever I go, You abide with me. Open not only my eyes but also my heart and soul to know Your revealed self. Create in me a desire to commune*

Sometimes I Forget

with You. Receive my sincere prayers and worship. With the help of the Holy Spirit, I come to You in spirit and in truth. Meet me there, dear Lord.

TRUTH REMINDER
Wherever I go,
God abides with me.

47. God Is Sanctifying

Sometimes I forget, Lord, that You are *sanctifying*, refining and purifying. . . .

> "Every branch in me that does not produce fruit he removes, and he prunes every branch that produces fruit so that it will produce more fruit." (John 15:2)

"Sanctification is the real change in man from the sordidness of sin to the purity of God's image."
WILLIAM AMES[53]

I recently read about a missionary pastor who served in Colombia with his family. The Good News was desperately needed in this war-torn drug haven. Corruption, violence, and drugs robbed the people of hope. A local guerrilla group controlled the area where the pastor ministered and the threats and persecution finally chased him and his family out. After some time of much-needed rest and renewal, they made an impossible decision. Despite great fear and trepidation, they decided to return to Colombia. This time they would tread deeper into the "red zone" to continue their ministry. Their choice amazed me. Everyone would have understood if they had decided to minister in a safer area of the country or leave altogether. In fact, his parents had begged him not to go in the first place. But he felt God's leading, so he packed up his family and headed in again despite the danger. Fear pursued him, but faith spurred him on.

Sometimes I Forget

I'm no missionary pastor, but I marvel at his choice and the choice of so many who put their lives on the line for the gospel. Where does such faith come from? How do we find the fortitude to take the news of Christ to the corners of the world or to our neighbor, for that matter? How do we gain the strength to willingly step into danger? How do we replace fear with faith? That's what this pastor had to do. Ultimately, how do we overcome the power of the flesh? This minister was afraid, but he had something more powerful driving him: the power of Christ.

As Christians, "little Christs," we reflect God's character, mirroring Him more accurately as He molds and refines us through the trials and circumstances of life. Through this process of sanctification, we grow in holiness and love. As we do, we receive God's supernatural strength. That's what gives martyrs the ability to cling to their faith when threatened with torture and death. Rev. Richard Wurmbrand, the minister in communist Romania whom we mentioned earlier, explains it this way: "If the heart is cleansed by the love of Jesus Christ, and if the heart loves Him, one can resist all tortures."[54]

Our flesh still sins. We still betray Him and always will to some extent as long as we walk in this human body. But, in Christ, we have victory over our flesh. Through His death and resurrection, He washed away our past filth and the filth to come from our very being—cleansing us and making us pure and holy to enter into the presence of His Father, to enter into His kingdom forever. Until then, He refines us, sometimes through the suffering we experience here, and we begin to take on a more Christlike appearance. Purified by trials and tribulations, we will walk and talk more like our Lord. We become more like Him—never in our strength, but always by the power of our Lord. Crucified with Christ, our heart begins to fear the temporal less while it desires to serve and glorify our Divine Creator more. It's a beautiful exchange and makes love possible in any situation.

Sometimes I Forget

Sometimes I forget, Lord, that You are sanctifying, refining and purifying. I forget that You use all I face to crucify my flesh and perfect me. Remind me that You desire to set me apart, to transform me, making me fit for Your holy purpose. Remind me that I can do nothing good and righteous without You; it is Your supernatural presence and power in me that enables me to love, to overcome fear, to obey. Sanctify me, Lord, change my heart and my mind. Do Your gracious work in me to make me holy.

TRUTH REMINDER
God uses all I face to perfect me
and make me more like Jesus.

48. God Is Wrathful

Sometimes I forget, Lord, that You are *wrathful*, exacting punishment on all that is unrighteous. . . .

> For we know the one who has said,
>
> > "Vengeance belongs to me; I will repay,"
>
> and again,
>
> > "The Lord will judge his people."
>
> It is a terrifying thing to fall into the hands of the living God. (Heb. 10:30–31)

"The bow of God's wrath is bent, and the arrow made ready on the string, and justice bends the arrow at your heart, and strains the bow, and it is nothing but the mere pleasure of God, and that of an angry God, without any promise or obligation at all, that keeps the arrow one moment from being made drunk with your blood."

JONATHAN EDWARDS[55]

The knot in my stomach tightened. Flipping between tabs and social media sites only added to my angst. Every news story, every video, showed the same thing: ugliness, hatred, fighting, fear, weeping, burning buildings, broken storefronts, pillaging. It appeared the world and everyone in it had gone mad, seemingly overnight. Violence and angry rhetoric had become a new norm, largely replacing compassion and civil dialogue. Adding to the mess, a mysterious virus terrorized the world, locking people in their homes for two years and robbing them of any sense of control.

Sometimes I Forget

Coming out of that, *self-expression* and *self-will* are the catchwords of the day. "Whatever feels good." "As long as it doesn't 'hurt' another." Greed, pride, and sexual sin seem to run rampant. God's love has been watered down to mean nothing; His holiness largely forgotten. It seems Western culture is beginning to view Christianity as a relic, antiquated and unneeded. Those who believe Scripture to be true and reliable receive ridicule and even hostility.

The faithful pray for revival. Believers rally, clinging to God's truth, reaching out to the lost, and encouraging each other. Still, discouragement is real. Evil appears to be winning. But it's not! And it never will. The Messiah will come to judge the earth.

The Lord loves all that is good and right, all that reflects His character. He is good, merciful, gracious, kind, and generous. But He intensely hates sin and will exact punishment and judgment for all unrighteousness, not as a cruel and sadistic being, but as a holy and righteous supreme being. Scripture provides accounts of God's wrath being exacted on those who sin against Him. He destroyed Sodom and Gomorrah for their sin (Gen. 19). He sent a flood to destroy all life except Noah, his family, and two of every animal and bird because of the great evil of the world (Gen. 6–8). God's wrath is real and must be satisfied.

Yes, the world may be going mad, and it may appear people are getting away with exercising all manner of evil. But appearances are often deceiving, and in this case, they are. God is sovereign; His will governs all. He may be disappointed by our sin, but He is not surprised by it. In His grace, He's exercising patience, wanting all to come to Him. But He will not force salvation on anyone, and He will not withhold His wrath forever. Christ promises to return and this time as a conquering warrior, bringing justice for every evil and punishment for every evildoer.

As Christians we don't need to fear God's wrath, but that doesn't mean it isn't coming. God is faithful. He acts according

Sometimes I Forget

to His unchanging, loving, holy, merciful, wrathful, and gracious nature. Although He desires all to be saved, He cannot let evil go unpunished. His wrath will come on those who reject His Son. For those of us who believe, though, the penalty has been paid. On the cross, Jesus Christ took the punishment for all who repent and receive Him as their Lord and Savior. We graciously receive forgiveness. The saving grace of Jesus protects all who trust in Him. As His followers, we already stand justified by His cleansing blood.

> *Sometimes I forget, Lord, that You are* wrathful, *exacting punishment on the unrighteous. I forget that You will judge the world. I grow weary and discouraged by the prevalence of evil in the world; it seems to be winning. Remind me, Lord, of Your holiness and wrath. Remind me that sin will not go unpunished. But lest I be paralyzed by fear, dear God, remind me also of how You saved me from Your awful judgment. Help me remember that, although Your wrath will come on the unrighteous, You already poured it out on Jesus Christ to save me and all who believe in Him as their Lord and Savior. Thank You, Lord! Help me be bold in sharing the truth about Your wrath and the good news of salvation in Christ.*

TRUTH REMINDER
God will pour out His wrath on the unrighteous, but I stand righteous by the saving grace of Jesus.

49. God Is Compassionate

Sometimes I forget, Lord, that You are *compassionate*, caring and helpful. . . .

> As a father has compassion on his children,
> so the LORD has compassion on those who fear him. (Ps. 103:13)

*"Man may dismiss compassion
from his heart, but God will never."*
WILLIAM COWPER[56]

I was near tears. Nothing seemed to work. We had tried for years, and our daughter had another accident. As I cleaned her up (as well as the floor), I begged God for relief. Would these messes define the future? Would she never understand what it means to go in the toilet?

My eyes searched hers as I fought for composure. I begged my sweet girl to understand and assured her she was old enough. Fourteen is, isn't it? My pleading voice fell away as confusion and concern for me filled her beautiful brown eyes. And as I knelt to clean her up, I received the sweetest gift. Bending down, Rachel brushed my face with a gentle kiss.

I melted. Her compassion erased much of my frustration and sorrow, filling me instead with love and promise. That's what compassion does. It fills us up when circumstances have emptied us. It salves a wounded heart and bolsters a weakened spirit. My girl demonstrates it so well. I've known others in my life who are

Sometimes I Forget

also stalwarts of compassion. My longtime pastor's wife came alongside me on a particularly difficult Sunday and reassured me I was exactly the mother Rachel needed. A dear friend bought me the comfiest pants before one of my oldest son's surgeries, which would require an overnight (or two) stay. Another dear friend sends me cards just to let me know she cares.

What a gift to have sympathetic and helpful people in our lives! An even greater gift is knowing we have a caring, sympathetic God. Although friends and family mean well, they don't always have the time, inclination, or awareness to reach out. We never have to worry about that with the Lord. None of our concerns go unnoticed or unaddressed by the Almighty. He is always aware of our cares and concerns. His compassion knows no bounds.

I love the way the lyrics of this beautiful song capture the truth of our compassionate God:

> If it matters to you, it matters to the Master
> He wants to share the burdens you bear
> Whisper peace when your world gets shattered
> If it's your greatest joy or your deepest pain
> Or you're really needing an answer
> If it matters to you, it matters to the Master.
> —"It Matters to the Master,"
> The Collingsworth Family[57]

Whatever your wants and needs, God cares. Whatever your concerns, you have a compassionate, sympathetic God to lend an ear. Whatever burden you're struggling to carry, He wants to help bear the weight. Because "If it matters to you, it matters to the Master."

Sometimes I Forget

Sometimes I forget, Lord, that You are compassionate, caring and helpful. I forget that You want what's ultimately best for me and that You are acting on my behalf. Remind me that things are not always how they seem. What appears good to me may actually hurt me in the end; what looks like a dead end may be the door to the answers I desire. Help me trust that You know best, and in your compassion, You offer what's best to me.

TRUTH REMINDER
God is ever compassionate, caring about
my plight and acting on my behalf.

50. God Is Immeasurable

Sometimes I forget, Lord, that You are *immeasurable*, defying limits of any kind. . . .

> Who has measured the waters in the hollow of his hand or marked off the heavens with the span of his hand? Who has gathered the dust of the earth in a measure or weighed the mountains on a balance and the hills on the scales? (Isa. 40:12)

> *Could we with ink the ocean fill,*
> *And were the skies of parchment made;*
> *Were every stalk on earth a quill,*
> *And every man a scribe by trade;*
> *To write the love of God above*
> *Would drain the ocean dry;*
> *Nor could the scroll contain the whole,*
> *Though stretched from sky to sky.*
> FREDERICK MARTIN LEHMAN[58]

The day dawned full of promise, but two hours later, it felt empty. Tears streamed down my face. Sobs stole my breath. My husband knew no words would help, so he simply held me. This wasn't a new pain nor a new loss. It had first appeared more than eighteen years ago, beginning with the words "developmental disability." It continued when we heard "lifelong genetic syndrome" and eventually

Sometimes I Forget

"mental retardation." All words associated with our daughter. All fresh stabs of pain.

Through the years, I've learned to manage the loss pretty well. After all, we still have our beautiful girl. And she's curious, loving, and goofy. But she's also stubborn, needy, and functionally nonverbal. Much of the time I do well with the glaring gap between the dream we had for our only daughter and the reality of our life with her. I find her childlike perspective on life refreshing. I cherish the snuggles and the sweet "mama" she frequently voices. I marvel at her ability to love anybody and everybody.

The sadness creeps in when I let down my guard and start dwelling on the demands her disability places on us, the developmental gap between her and her peers, the things other moms experience with their daughters that I'm missing out on, and the fear for her future when her dad and I are no longer around. My joy and peace dissipate when I stare too long at what I wish would have been, what I think I'm missing out on, and what I fear coming up. Such shortsightedness births discontent and sorrow.

I'm looking at my situation in light of the here and now, the confines of this one hundred years of life. But God is immeasurable. Nothing confines Him to such a timetable. His vision extends infinitely. His is an eternal perspective.

True, our expectations in this life will never be fully met. But those shattered dreams and unfulfilled desires don't negate the beauty that does exist nor the beauty to come. We serve a God of redemption. A faithful God who pours out blessings on His children. A loving Father who shares our pain, catches our tears, and gives us a reality that always holds beauty. His plan isn't confined to today or tomorrow. He looks through a lens of endless tomorrows. He stretches fulfillment and abundance across a canvas of eternity. His is an immeasurable reality, defying all limits.

I expect this won't be the last time I weep over my daughter. But thanks to God's grace and mercy, it's not nearly as often as I

Sometimes I Forget

love over her and laugh with her . . . especially as I remind myself that God's reality for our lives nearly always looks different from what we envision. He works in mysterious ways far beyond our comprehension. So although this isn't the plan I had for Rachel, I'm asking God to help me see our reality as He does: in light of eternity. I'm learning to rest in His immeasurable understanding and His everlasting love. It's how we mine for lasting treasure we can't readily see.

> *Sometimes I forget, Lord, that You are* immeasurable, *defying limits of any kind. I forget that it is foolish to box You into a space of my understanding. When I do, I'm left wanting. Remind me, please, of Your eternal perspective, that You aren't confined to my understanding of the future. Remind me that You work in mysterious ways far beyond my comprehension. You gauge good while looking through a lens of endless tomorrows. You stretch fulfillment and abundance across a canvas of eternity. Help me rest, Lord, in Your immeasurable understanding and everlasting love.*

TRUTH REMINDER
God's perfect plan for my life flows from His limitless understanding and everlasting love.

51. God Is Sustaining

Sometimes I forget, Lord, that You are *sustaining*, supporting and upholding all You have created. . . .

"Give us today our daily bread." (Matt. 6:11)

"Don't you know that day dawns after night, showers displace drought, and spring and summer follow winter? Then, have hope! Hope forever, for God will not fail you!"
—CHARLES SPURGEON[59]

It had been a tumultuous birth, and more than a week passed before we could bring our firstborn home. I so wanted to be brave, but the moment we laid him down I was met with apprehension and insecurity. My joy over this little guy's life remained, but my confidence evaporated as my husband and I looked at each other across the bed, the weight of responsibility hanging between us.

Now what? Here we were, this precious week-old life and two seemingly ill-equipped, unprepared adults. Questions assailed my mind: How could we offer all Daniel needed to grow strong and healthy in mind, body, and soul? What if we did this parenting thing all wrong? How would he survive our mistakes? Were we up for this lifelong commitment?

The answers scared me more than the questions. We couldn't offer him all he needed. We would do things wrong. We would be lacking. We could never be up to meeting the demands of such a huge commitment.

Sometimes I Forget

But through the past nearly thirty years of parenting, I saw that where we fell short, God filled in. In our dearth, He provided abundance. When we lacked courage, He gave us His.

By God's grace alone, those earlier questions were answered in glorious ways. He provided what we could not. He placed others in our lives to offer parenting wisdom. His grace covered our mistakes. He carried us when our strength failed. And He even provided the courage when I didn't know how to be brave.

The Lord supports and upholds not only His children, but all of His creation. He keeps the earth spinning and the sun and moon moving. He maintains the natural cycles and controls the changing of seasons. He preserves life and provides for all its needs. God sustains with an unsurpassed power.

So it frustrates me when I give into doubt and fear when faced with something difficult or unknown. I act like it all falls on my shoulders to figure it out and power through. I look into the future and wonder how I can survive for that long. But Jesus counsels us to not "worry about tomorrow, because tomorrow will worry about itself. Each day has enough trouble of its own" (Matt. 6:34). And He taught us to pray: "Give us today our daily bread" (v. 11). In His grace, God will provide all we need for today. Tomorrow He will provide fresh grace.

The Lord wanted the Israelites to trust in His sustaining power in the desert, so He provided them with a test:

> Then the LORD said to Moses, "I am going to rain bread from heaven for you. The people are to go out each day and gather enough for that day. This way I will test them to see whether or not they will follow my instructions. On the sixth day, when they prepare what they bring in, it will be twice as much as they gather on other days." (Exod. 16:4–5)

Sometimes I Forget

He would provide only enough food for each day, with one exception. The day before Sabbath, they could gather enough for that day and Sabbath. The test was to teach them to rely on God for life and living. They failed.

I know the Almighty is a sustaining God, but sadly, I'm not very good at passing His tests either. Like the Israelites, I've experienced the Lord's support in many ways throughout my life, but I still often fail to trust Him with the next hurdle. By the grace of God, though, and with the help of the Holy Spirit, I am growing in faith. When I remember that His daily bread is more than abundant for today, I feel the pressure slide right off my shoulders. What a glorious way to live!

Sometimes I forget, Lord, that You are sustaining, supporting and upholding all You have created. I forget that You provide for all of Your creation, including me. When a trial comes along, I foolishly believe I need to shoulder through on my own strength. Remind me, Lord, that You will supply all I need for this day, and that You will have fresh grace for tomorrow. Remind me that You sustain all with unsurpassed power, never growing weak or weary. Thank You, Lord! Help me accept Your provisions and release the pressure of carrying it all on my own shoulders. Help me trust You to provide where I lack.

TRUTH REMINDER
God supports and maintains all of creation, including me, providing me with all I need for each day.

52. God Is Free

Sometimes I forget, Lord, that You are *free*, not bound to the dictates of anyone or anything. . . .

> Our God is in heaven
> and does whatever he pleases. (Ps. 115:3)

> *"True and absolute freedom is only
> found in the presence of God."*
> A. W. TOZER[60]

Watching Rachel tug on the undershirt, I soon realized it was caught on her ID bracelet. She kept tugging. Pull as she might, though, she could not get the shirt off. Realizing her mounting frustration, I intervened.

"Pull it back first, Rach," I counseled.

Because sometimes we have to pull back before we can move forward. Pull back from our anger to move toward forgiveness. Pull back from self-righteousness to move toward God's righteousness. Pull back from the bondage of sin to experience the freedom of Christ.

"That's it. If you pull it back first, it'll let go," I encouraged.

Because we may need to release before we can reap. Release our understanding to reap the peace of the Holy Spirit. Release our expectations to reap the joy of the Father. Release our desires to reap the freedom of Christ.

As she pulled the shirt back up her arm, opposite the way she wanted it to go, it broke free. Once free from the bracelet, the

Sometimes I Forget

shirt pulled easily off Rachel's arm. And a cheer sprung from our lips. Because freedom is always worth celebrating. Even freedom from a stubborn shirt.

Here in the United States of America we pride ourselves on being the land of the free. But many abuse that liberty, using it to suppress others or feed their own sinful choices. In fact, all humanity acts in opposition to what is morally good and right. That's not what our Creator had in mind for us. He wanted us to be free to glorify Him in all of our words and actions—an impossible feat now, given our flawed nature.

God desires for us to spend eternity in His presence, to enjoy and celebrate creation with Him. But that requires a righteous and holy heart, far from what any of us have in our fallen state. Our sins hold us in bondage.

Unlike us, God is divinely free; He has no bounds or constraints. And in His infinite love, grace, and mercy, He desires to unbind us from our shackles. So He gives to us from His divine freedom, His well of liberty. Not as a mandate but as a gift. The Lord sent His Son to break our bonds, bust down the prison doors, and set us free.

Out of His divine nature, God gives us relative freedom to make choices pleasing to Him or to refuse His grace. If we reject His offer, He will still use us for His purposes here on earth, but we'll be imprisoned for all eternity. Accept Christ by faith through His grace, and we walk in freedom forever.

Like Rachel being released from her undershirt, the Lord's gift of freedom means we can move forward. Bought with the blood of Jesus on the cross, it ushers us into a life of greater purpose. When poured out on us, the Lord's freedom allows us to reap the rewards of the life we were created to live and to spend eternity with Christ. And that's the kind of freedom always worth celebrating!

Sometimes I Forget

Sometimes I forget, Lord, that You are free, not bound to the dictates of anyone or anything. I forget that You are not constrained in ways I would expect, so I put limits on what You can and will do. Remind me that You've poured out Your freedom on me, rescuing me from the shackles of sin. Comfort me in that, although I regularly fail You, You can even use my transgressions as instruments of Your grace. You allow Your creation to exercise free will, but You still have ultimate control and overrule the freedom of all as You see fit. I'm grateful You secured salvation for me and broke the bonds of my sin. Help me walk in Your freedom as I remember that a beautiful eternity awaits me in the finished and complete work of Jesus Christ.

TRUTH REMINDER
In Christ, I am free to walk out a life
of great purpose and meaning.

53. God Is Miraculous

Sometimes I forget, Lord, that You are *miraculous*, acting beyond the realm of human understanding and ability. . . .

> You are the God who performs miracles;
> you display your power among the peoples.
> (Ps. 77:14 NIV)

"It is not the objective proof of God's existence that we want but the experience of God's presence. That is the miracle we are really after, and that is also, I think, the miracle that we really get."
FREDERICK BUECHNER[61]

I love caroling. Our boys . . . not so much. Our church ladies' group had planned an evening of Christmas caroling at the local nursing and assisted-living homes. Although I cannot really be classified as a singer, I love to worship in that form and do make a joyful noise. Always eager to encourage my boys to bless others with their gifts of voice, I convinced them to join us women, promising cookies and punch afterward. (That seldom fails!)

It was a nice evening, as I expected. The boys added some appreciated variety to our female voices, and Rachel waved to everyone she saw. Many ladies wanted to shake Rach's hand and/or give her a hug. She readily complied; I even had to pry her away a few times. About halfway through our time at the nursing home, a wheelchair-bound lady began wheeling along with us, joining in song, and encouraging Rachel to hold her hand. She even pointed out her room to us; "Irene" was written on the door.

Sometimes I Forget

When our time finally came to leave that facility for the next stop, Irene lingered. She seemed reluctant to see us go. The children and I were the last ones out (Rachel's a little slow at the coat thing . . . and the saying goodbye thing . . . and the doing-as-she-is-told thing). And her unhurried nature is precisely why God uses her in such profound ways.

The exchange that took place next convinced me that what I perceived as an ordinary night of caroling had taken on miraculous significance. With a final "Merry Christmas" and "Thanks for singing with us," we turned to leave. A voice choked with emotion reclaimed our attention. Irene informed us that her husband had died that year, and the holidays were tough. With tears threatening to spill over, she explained that it brought her much joy to sing with us; it was just what she needed to help her through the pain and loneliness.

In that moment, our caroling became anything but "normal." It took on a sacredness of blessing others and being blessed. It seemed God didn't just bring our group to the nursing home at that time to bring a little cheer and love. He placed us there to be His arms to hug one of His hurting children. He orchestrated our presence, so that we could be His voice, singing life back into an elderly lady's withering spirit.

During that night of caroling so many years ago, God used a mixed group of carolers to unwrap the gift of Jesus Christ, the Almighty Incarnate, for many lonely residents—one lady in particular. What began as an ordinary night of caroling became a "miraculous" event of experiencing Immanuel—God with Us!

Our hallowed night hinted at God's miraculous nature. The expression of this wondrous aspect of God's nature appears throughout the pages of Scripture: God speaking to Moses out of a burning bush that never burned up (Exod. 3–4); the parting of the Red Sea (Exod. 14:21); and the miraculous provision of manna for the wandering Israelites (Exod. 16). Miracles conducted by

Sometimes I Forget

Jesus fill the Gospels: giving sight to the blind (Mark 10:46–52), healing the lame (Matt. 9:1–8), raising the dead (Matt. 9:18–26). He used these works of His hands to reveal Himself, to demonstrate His love, and to heal and restore. But the most wondrous miracle of all occurred more than two thousand years ago on a hill called Golgotha, when the incarnate Son of God died on the cross to defeat death itself (Matt. 27), having repercussions for eternity.

Although they don't seem to be as prevalent, the Lord continues to do miracles today: the sudden disappearance of stage 4 cancer tumors, living through an "unsurvivable" car accident, the survival of an aborted baby. Miracles are an "ordinary" part of His nature. But to us, they point to the divine, reminding us of where our hope lies and allowing us to experience His presence in the greatest miracle of all: God's forgiveness of our sins and adoption into His family!

> *Sometimes I forget, Lord, that You are* miraculous, *acting beyond the realm of human understanding and ability. I forget that You often operate outside of what's natural or possible. I expect the ordinary, but You offer me much more, sanctifying me and giving me glimpses of Your wondrous nature as You work in my life. Remind me that You aren't limited by the powers of nature or the understanding of man; You transcend all creation. Help me notice Your works in the ordinary as well as the miraculous. Remind me of Your greatest miracle those many centuries ago that continues to give life to the lost.*

TRUTH REMINDER
God is always present and working in my life
in mysterious and miraculous ways.

54. God Is Joyful

Sometimes I forget, Lord, that You are *joyful*, filled with delight and gladness. . . .

> But let all who take refuge in you rejoice;
> let them shout for joy forever.
> May you shelter them,
> and may those who love your name boast
> about you. (Ps. 5:11)

*"Joy is not the absence of suffering
but the presence of God."*
JANET ERSKINE STUART[62]

Sunlight danced on the walls as I struggled to keep my eyes open. In those twilight moments between deep sleep and fully awake, a film reel kept running through my mind. It featured concerns of the past days and apprehension at the coming ones. But breaking into that stream like sunlight through clouds came thoughts of Jesus and light.

Jesus is the light. He brings joy and security. Joy and security, peace amid struggles, a sense of well-being when life hurts. In the hush of the early morning, my semiconscious mind came to rest there and held on for dear life.

It had been a difficult season. "Let's just run away," I had begged my husband, "just for a couple nights. Please!" Yet I knew that wasn't reasonable or possible.

Sometimes I Forget

Responsibilities kept piling on. Hurts kept adding up. Getting away wasn't on the table, so I turned to other means of salving the pain and exhaustion I felt. Shows, music, hobbies, chores—nothing seemed to do the trick. In fact, they only stretched my nerves further because, as I filled my days with activities and distractions, I masked the joy I already had in Christ.

We often confuse happiness and joy. Happiness is experience-driven while joy transcends our experiences. Happiness depends on external influences. Joy exists as the delight and fulfillment of spirit, a deep peace, and that comes from our relationship with the triune God.

As Christians, we already have the joy of the Lord, and we glorify Him when we reflect it. But when life becomes chaotic, we often look to *make* joy instead of abiding in the One whose being is joy.

The Bible clearly articulates where our joy comes from: "He [God] will yet fill your mouth with laughter and your lips with a shout of joy" (Job 8:21); "LORD, you are my portion and my cup of blessing; . . . in your presence is abundant joy" (Ps. 16:5a–b, 11b); "Rejoice in the Lord always. I will say it again: Rejoice!" (Phil. 4:4). Created in community, our souls find delight in communion with our Creator. Our relationship with the Lord gladdens our spirit.

So instead of looking to manufacture joy when we find ourselves overwhelmed, worn out, and anxious, we can remind ourselves of who is the author of joy. We can thank God for the Holy Spirit. And we can look to the light of Christ to break through the fog, allowing us to experience the joy . . . right in the middle of the chaos.

Sometimes I forget, Lord, that You are joyful, filled with delight and gladness. I forget that I can't make joy, that it exists as a fulfillment of spirit, a deep peace. Remind me that I can still have joy in the middle of the chaos and hurt because it is not based on

Sometimes I Forget

my experiences or circumstances. Remind me that You are its source and that I can receive it by knowing and abiding in You and being filled with Your Spirit. Help me bring You glory, Lord, as I reflect Your joy during those most painful seasons.

TRUTH REMINDER
God provides joy, even in the
middle of chaos and hurt.

55. God Is Approachable

Sometimes I forget, Lord, that You are *approachable*, unveiled and welcoming. . . .

> Therefore, let us approach the throne of grace with boldness, so that we may receive mercy and find grace to help us in time of need. (Heb. 4:16)

"Always, everywhere God is present, and always He seeks to discover Himself. To each one he would reveal not only that He is, but what He is as well."

A. W. TOZER[63]

"Dave, you need to come back now." I choked out the words. "They're taking him away!"

Our son had been born a few hours earlier after a twenty-three-and-a-half-hour labor. After that long, drawn-out ordeal, he was delivered into the cold and sterile delivery room. His lusty cry greeted us—but so did a confusing sight. Daniel had experienced birth or in-utero trauma to his left arm. His arm, extremely swollen, had sores scattered from the elbow joint to the base of his thumb. None of the attending medical staff knew what to do about it.

Finally, after the doctors and nurses stabilized Daniel, my husband retired to our house for a few hours of much-needed sleep. My call pulled him out of his exhausted slumber. Near hysteria, I drew a deep breath before once again trying to help my groggy husband understand.

"They're afraid Daniel's sores might be infected and want to life-flight him to Omaha. I can't go; you have to come now!"

Wide-awake by now, Dave hurried back. He arrived just in time to see our little guy off in the helicopter. Exhaustion and concern creased his face. We talked briefly before he followed in the car with my heart, but not the rest of me, in tow. Unable to be released from the hospital after such a long labor and with an unknown rash, my desperate prayer had to suffice.

The next day found me staring through the tiny windows of a Neonatal Intensive Care Unit (NICU) door at my precious little boy in the arms of his daddy. With my first pregnancy ending in a miscarriage, this seemed to be another cruel twist. I longed to take him in my arms, but hadn't yet received the all-clear on my rash. It took all the self-discipline I possessed not to push through those doors, rash or not.

It was one of the longest days of my life. For twenty-four hours a barrier prevented me from visiting my newborn; first distance, then a NICU door. Finally, after what felt like a lifetime, I received permission to draw near to my son. Few things could have been sweeter.

The Israelites saw a barrier as well. During the time they wandered in the desert, God had them construct a portable tabernacle and carry it with them. This served as a place of worship, a place to meet the Lord. However, only the high priest could enter the inner room, the Holy of Holies, where the very presence of God dwelled. And even he only entered once a year on Yom Kippur (the Day of Atonement). A curtain separated this chamber from the rest of the tabernacle, keeping sinners from entering into God's presence. Whenever the Israelites went to worship, they were separated from God by the curtain.

Sometimes I Forget

A similar setup existed in the Jerusalem temple, the temple that stood during Jesus's crucifixion. Upon Jesus's death, when He "cried out again with a loud voice and gave up his spirit . . . the curtain of the sanctuary was torn in two from top to bottom" (Matt. 27:50–51). The curtain, the veil, was torn! It no longer barred people from entering into the presence of the Lord. It opened up direct access to Him. This means we can again approach God. We can fellowship directly with Him. We don't need to fear drawing near. As sinners cleansed with the blood of Jesus, we have His righteousness, and a barrier no longer separates us. We can approach the throne of grace with confidence—and we should.

The sacrifice of Christ on the cross, His death, not only tore the veil of separation in the temple, but it bridged the chasm that separated us from God and cloaked us in Christ's righteousness so we could dwell in God's presence. It made God approachable to man again. It gave us access to God, to be strengthened, encouraged, and restored. And that plays an essential role in navigating this broken world.

Sometimes I forget, Lord, that You are approachable, unveiled and welcoming. I forget that You are both within reach and far above anything I can understand, so I hesitate to come near. Remind me, Lord, that the barrier separating us has been torn in two. Help me feel free to approach Your throne of grace in reverence and humility, with questions and doubts, with requests and thanksgiving. Because of Jesus's death on the cross, You no longer see my sin, but instead, You see His righteousness. Please wipe away all shame, fear, and hesitancy on my part and draw me into Your presence.

Sometimes I Forget

TRUTH REMINDER
God welcomes me into His presence, seeing Christ's righteousness instead of my sin.

56. God Is Generous

Sometimes I forget, Lord, that You are *generous*, lavish in giving. . . .

> "If you then, who are evil, know how to give good gifts to your children, how much more will your Father in heaven give good things to those who ask him." (Matt. 7:11)

"The heart that is generous and kind most resembles God."
ROBERT BURNS[64]

A couple of years ago my youngest befriended an elderly lady in our local nursing home. We visited her a time or two, and on Valentine's Day of that year my son decided to gift her with a little teddy bear. He spent time picking out just the right gift, one he felt would help her feel special and cared for. We placed it in a cute little bag and went to deliver it.

Unfortunately, our friend moved to an out-of-town nursing home before we could gift it to her, so we left it in the home for the staff to give to another lonely resident. The bear was nothing extravagant, but I'm certain it had a large impact on the recipient. Why? Because it said you are not forgotten, because it conveyed that someone cared, because it came from my son's heart.

I'm proud of Joey's generosity. He gave out of love, a reflection of the generosity and love our Father bestows on us. Giving is a beautiful way to glorify and bless the Lord. But we're never going to out-give the maker of our souls.

Sometimes I Forget

God is generous by nature. He daily showers us with blessings. He lavishes us with opportunities, relationships, and provisions. He placed the stars in the sky and painted the world with color. He provided every manner of creature for our use and pleasure. He sowed flowers of many hues. He gives us friends and family members. He supplies warmth and rain. He created us with senses for which to delight in creation.

These are all gifts. He doesn't wait for us to earn any of it. My son didn't expect his elderly friend to pay for the teddy bear. He wanted to gift it to her as a reminder that he cared for her. Similarly, God doesn't expect payment for His generosity. He isn't waiting for us to scrape up enough goodness. He heaps blessings on us simply because He loves and cares for us.

We don't have to wonder if God's generosity will run out or if He'll become stingy with it. God's nature does not change. He will not become less than what He is now. His thoughtfulness will span the generations until it culminates in a new heaven and new earth! The God whose generosity and grace spilled over in offering us the gift of eternal life "while we were still sinners" (Rom. 5:8) never changes and will never run low on blessings to impart.

God is an endless well of generosity. He gives to us freely from His abundance. It's a beautiful thing when we respond to others in kind.

Sometimes I forget, Lord, that You are generous, lavish in giving. I forget that You delight in sharing Your abundance with me. Remind me of Your great thoughtfulness in creating variety and beauty, family and friends, seasons and opportunities. Remind me that You bless me out of Your great love, expecting only gratitude in return. And reassure me, Lord, that as an endless well of generosity, You'll never run out of gifts or grow tired of gifting me.

Sometimes I Forget

I'm so grateful! May I, in turn, bring You glory through my own generosity toward others.

TRUTH REMINDER
God delights in giving me
good and abundant gifts.

57. God Is Personal

Sometimes I forget, Lord, that You are *personal*, living and self-aware. . . .

> But the LORD is the true God;
> he is the living God and eternal King.
> The earth quakes at his wrath,
> and the nations cannot endure his fury.
> (Jer. 10:10)

"We did not seek You, but You sought us; we did not come to You, but You came to us. You saw us lying in the blood of our sins, and behold, Your heart broke, and You said to us: 'You shall live!'"

C. F. W. WALTHER[65]

We awoke early to catch the train from Bangkok to Ayutthaya, the abandoned capital of the Siamese Kingdom. I slid into a window seat and tried to rub the filth off the glass. My two oldest boys occupied spots next to me. As we passed a small station in remote Thailand, I spotted a man sitting on a worn wooden bench, bags scattered around his feet. On his lap nestled a boy I guessed to be around ten years old. The child's legs stuck straight out. He was obviously crippled and appeared to have intellectual disabilities as well. The affection of the father captivated me as he tenderly and repeatedly kissed his son's face. I couldn't tear my gaze away from them, watching until the train took us out of view.

Such a tender love. This man appeared to be alone, perhaps taking his son to a doctor appointment, a relative's home, or any number of places. Traveling alone with his son couldn't have been easy, but clearly this father's love ran deep.

It's also how I picture our Father in heaven. The Lord is a personal God, one who stays in relation with His creation, not some impersonal entity who created us only to leave us alone to fend for ourselves. Our God is one who perfectly and righteously expresses emotions, not being affected by outside influences but acting in accordance with all His other attributes. He loves us with an everlasting love. He thinks, plans, and makes choices. He wills and acts on that will. He creates, shepherds, and sustains.

As a being created in His image, we reflect God's character. So it shouldn't surprise us when we come across an instance as tender as the Thai father and his son. It was obvious that man would do anything for his child, including lay down his life. In an expression of His personhood, that's exactly what the Lord has done for us. Only our Savior gave up His life not just for one, but for all who have faith—an expression of love and mercy that knows no bounds.

Sometimes I forget, Lord, that You are personal, living and self-aware. I forget that You are a rational being capable of thought, will, and interaction with me. Remind me of Your personhood, wisdom, goodness, sense of justice, and even Your righteous anger. Remind me of Your holiness but also of the depth of Your love and mercy, reflected in Jesus Christ's restoration and renewal of my sin-laden life through His death and resurrection. Guide me in my thoughts and actions, so I carry out Your will, glorifying You in the way I live.

TRUTH REMINDER
God willed and acted to bring me into relationship with Him and will guide me in reasoning and living out my life.

58. God Is Foreknowing

Sometimes I forget, Lord, that You are *foreknowing*, having known and loved me from eternity. . . .

> For those he foreknew he also predestined to be conformed to the image of his Son, so that he would be the firstborn among many brothers and sisters. And those he predestined, he also called; and those he called, he also justified; and those he justified, he also glorified. (Rom. 8:29–30)
>
> *"Everyone who believes in God at all believes that He knows what you and I are going to do tomorrow."*
> —C. S. LEWIS[66]

Born with a birth injury to his left arm, our oldest son had a buildup of scar tissue and reduced utility in that limb. Therapy had helped, but it still wasn't functional.

On the recommendation of Daniel's pediatrician, my husband and I decided to take our eight-month-old son to a doctor in Houston, Texas, who specialized in orthopedics. This specialist was recommended as an expert in his profession. We hoped he could advise us as to whether surgery would help restore additional mobility and use.

The trip proved to be disastrous in many respects: an arrogant doctor with poor bedside manners; no worthwhile recommendations; and a rotavirus that ravaged our son's little body and made the one-thousand-mile drive home a nightmare.

Our son's arm did require surgery several years later. In fact, he underwent two surgeries for it. Unfortunately, it never did become fully functional. As difficult as this experience was, I now see God's hand in it.

Daniel's injured arm didn't surprise the Lord; God wasn't left wondering what had gone wrong. In His foreknowledge, He knew about the birth defect before Daniel was born, before he was even conceived. He foreknew our struggles in Texas and the later surgeries. He was aware of the limitations our son would have because of it. In fact, God wasn't only conscious of it, the whole thing came around according to His counsel and will. That's comforting.

It is a blessing to know we are not at the mercy of chance, that God has His hand in the happenings of our lives. The Lord's foreknowing also assures a benefit will come from our difficult circumstances if we receive it. Daniel did; he accepted his arm limitations. In return, he found areas of interest and things he excelled in that he might not have otherwise.

Foreknowing is a difficult attribute to grasp given our finite understanding. Theologians differ on its exact meaning and application. But Scripture is clear that God isn't in the dark when it comes to the future (or anything else, for that matter). And knowing the Lord meets us there is a great mercy.

> *Sometimes I forget, Lord, that You are* foreknowing, *having known and loved me from eternity. I forget that You know my actions before I do them and my thoughts before I think them. How foolish to think I can hide something from You. Remind me, Lord, of the agency of my prayers—that You answer before I utter them. Remind me of the great love You must have for me that You*

Sometimes I Forget

thought of me and chose me to be Yours before I was born. And when a trial comes, Lord, help me remember that it is according to Your counsel and will, and that You will bring benefit from it.

TRUTH REMINDER
I am not at the mercy of chance; God knows all about my future and has His hand in all the happenings of my life.

59. God Is Shepherding

Sometimes I forget, Lord, that You are *shepherding*, guiding, directing, and protecting me. . . .

> The LORD is my shepherd;
> I have what I need. (Ps. 23:1)

> *"I know not the way God leads me,*
> *but well do I know my Guide."*
> MARTIN LUTHER[67]

It had been a particularly difficult Sunday when, in tears, I confessed to my pastor's wife: "I don't know how to raise Rachel. I can't do this! I don't know how to care for a child with special needs."

I didn't then and I still don't. But in the ensuing years, I've had an important truth about God reinforced: He isn't only a God above us, He's also a God with us. We sing about that truth at Christmas: "Immanuel . . . 'God is with us'" (Matt. 1:23). But when the hymn ends, many of us continue to live like we need to fend for ourselves in this vast universe. Scripture tells us a different story.

God is definitely above and beyond us, but He's also with us and in us (for believers). "I am the good shepherd," Jesus claimed (John 10:14a). "I know my own, and my own know me" (v. 14b). The Good Shepherd knows us, and He walks with us through this life. He provides all we need, including giving us life (Ps. 23:1). He helps us flourish (v. 2). He renews and strengthens us (v. 3). He protects and comforts us (v. 4). He fills our cup to overflowing with blessings and keeps us near (vv. 5–6).

Early in our journey with disabilities, I lost sight of hope. So the Lord connected me with a friend who told me about a wonderful treatment program that helped me see our daughter as a gift. Later, with no support group available because Rachel didn't have a diagnosis, God planted a seed of an idea and I banded together with a school counselor to lead a support group of my own. When the isolation and loneliness of caring for my daughter grew, the Lord joined me to a network of parents who understand the complexities, joys, and struggles of life with differently abled children, and who were being trained to actively educate others. This led me to begin speaking, which contrary to anything I could have imagined at the time, was the genesis for my writing.

God knew I didn't have a clue on how to parent a child with special needs or the strength to do it. He also knew I'd be hesitant to encourage others with all He was teaching me. So he set about directing my steps. Like a shepherd leading his sheep, the Lord led me. Looking back, I clearly see the path He took me on.

Like sheep look to their shepherd for guidance and provision, the Lord wants us to look to Him. He'll make a way. He will light the path. He'll carry us when we don't have the strength to continue. And when we're lost, He'll come looking for us. That's what shepherds do. How much more will the Good Shepherd do?

Sometimes I forget, Lord, that You are shepherding, guiding, directing, and protecting me. I forget that instead of remaining only above and beyond me, You are with me. Remind me that You are the Good Shepherd, leading me through life. Your commands and warnings are for my own good. Remind me that when I lose my way, You will find me and guide me back, and when I grow

Sometimes I Forget

weary, You will carry me. Reassure me, Lord, that I can trust You to provide all I need.

TRUTH REMINDER
God is with me, guiding me through
life and providing what I need.

60. God Is Redemptive

Sometimes I forget, Lord, that You are *redemptive*, restoring all creation. . . .

> Then I saw a new heaven and a new earth; for the first heaven and the first earth had passed away, and the sea was no more. I also saw the holy city, the new Jerusalem, coming down out of heaven from God, prepared like a bride adorned for her husband.
> Then I heard a loud voice from the throne: Look, God's dwelling is with humanity, and he will live with them. They will be his peoples, and God himself will be with them and will be their God. He will wipe away every tear from their eyes. Death will be no more; grief, crying, and pain will be no more, because the previous things have passed away. (Rev. 21:1–4)

"When Christ shall come with shout of acclamation
And take me home, what joy shall fill my heart!
Then I shall bow in humble adoration,
And there proclaim, 'My God, how great Thou art!'"

STUART K. HINE[68]

My daughter cannot run, at least not in the true sense of the word. She can't get both feet off the ground at the same time. So in the past when we wanted to jog together, I'd strap her into a specially

Sometimes I Forget

adapted tricycle, and we would head for the campground roads near our home. We enjoyed getting out.

But ever since Rachel was little, I've held onto a special dream of us running together. My dream is set on a hill-top glade in Wisconsin. The trees perfectly encircle the clearing and the tall grass waves in the gentle breeze. Sun shining bright, my daughter and I join hands and start running through the meadow, hair flowing behind us and pure joy lighting our faces. Although Rach and I won't run together on earth, I love to think our hand-in-hand running will be a dream come true in heaven.

This does not have to be a pipe dream, thanks to Jesus Christ's atoning work on the cross. When Adam and Eve disobeyed God, they brought guilt and condemnation to all people. A holy God cannot be in the presence of sin. However, He wanted none to perish, so He put His plan of salvation into place. Jesus Christ voluntarily humbled Himself to die on the cross for the forgiveness of sins. He redeemed all people, buying us back from sin and death.

And when the Lamb of God returns again on the clouds, He will establish the new heavens and a new earth. All will be restored. There will be no more suffering—no more grief, pain, or sin. All who have been washed in the blood of the Lamb will then have access to the tree of life and be welcomed into the kingdom, where we will reign forever and ever.

Thank God, us Christians don't have to wonder where we will spend eternity. We'll be home in the new Jerusalem in unbroken fellowship with the Lord. And there we will all have new glorified bodies. Just imagine! No more tears. No more sickness. The blind will see, the deaf will hear, and the lame will leap for joy (Isa. 35:5–6). And Rachel? She will be able to run and skip with the best of them! Thanks to the shed blood of Jesus that will usher in the new creation, my dream of one day running hand in hand with my daughter will become reality in the new "Eden."

Sometimes I Forget

Sometimes I forget, Lord, that You are redemptive, restoring all creation. I forget that one day all will be new. You will create a new and permanent "Eden" where there will be no more grief, crying, or pain. Remind me that we live in a broken world of sin and death, but that You bring life. Remind me that Jesus Christ died to redeem to new life all who accept the free gift of salvation. Thank You, Lord, that on Christ's return, death will be no more; we will be whole and complete in our new glorified bodies. Thank You that we will then reign with You forever and ever. Amen!

TRUTH REMINDER
One day I will live in the new Jerusalem where there will be no grief, no sin, and no pain.

Conclusion: Hope Is There in the Furnace of Affliction

*"I asked for strength and God gave me
difficulties to make me strong.
I asked for wisdom and God gave me problems
to learn to solve.
I asked for prosperity and God gave me
a brain and brawn to work.
I asked for courage and God gave me dangers to overcome.
I asked for love and God gave me people to help.
I asked for favors and God gave me opportunities.
I received nothing I wanted.
I received everything I needed."*

HAZRAT INAYAT KHAN[69]

In a journal entry some years back, I called out to the Lord in distress:

> Oh Lord, the day weighs heavy! What should be happy brings tears anew. My heart hurts; sadness descends. Why? I'm uncertain, but it assaults in waves.
>
> Joy pokes and prods to surface, but the weightiness of despair pushes it back under.
>
> Yet, You, Lord, are there—always faithful, always loving. You are my hope when my spirit

> grows weary. Praise will be on my lips even as tears slide down my cheeks.
>
> Lord, I can't do this, what you ask of me. It is so hard and so lonely. I'm not sure I can carry this cross.
>
> But then, I'm not alone, am I?
>
> The image of You stumbling, crawling, clawing Your way up the hill carrying Your own impossible cross comes to my mind. Agony ripping through Your flesh.
>
> And then the worst—the complete separation from Your Father—utterly alone!
>
> You did it. You endured it. All for me!
>
> I can't carry this cross . . . but I don't have to, do I? For You carried it for me.
>
> In You I trust, Lord, even through my tears.
>
> Where else is there any hope?
>
> Hope . . . only in Your undying love!

Hope—that thing we all need for our souls to flourish. All of God is hope! We see it when we explore His character. We experience it as we walk with Him in faith. And we can believe it when the furnace of affliction lights up.

Coming back from our honeymoon more than thirty years ago, my husband and I swung through Yellowstone National Park. Earlier that summer, a forest fire had raged through a large section of the park. The recent inferno's devastation shocked us. Educated as fish and wildlife biologists, we both knew the benefits of fire for a forest. Lush growth would sprout from the ashes. But with such extensive damage, we struggled to accept that truth because we couldn't immediately see the blessing. What looked to be bad masked the promise of good.

Similarly, I look at the difficult things in my life and wrestle with the idea of a positive outcome. But looking back through the years, the good becomes apparent as I see life sprouting from the ashes. That's why Christians so often hear the mantra, "Walk by faith, not by sight" (2 Cor. 5:7). We're often not far enough removed from the fire to see the new growth, not far enough removed from our trials to see the promise fulfilled.

A hope-filled perspective takes time to develop. We need to grow in faith. Being in the Word and studying the character of God is a powerful way to do that. As we look at the Creator, our perspective on life can't help but shift as we get a big-picture view.

Although certain aspects of God's nature are readily apparent, such as His love, majesty, and mercy, others remain inscrutable. It seems the more we learn about Him the less we know. Oddly, that brings comfort, because the glorious, omnipotent, infinite Lord of the universe shouldn't be fully understandable.

Still, as we learn more about our Creator, we discover a solid foundation on which to place our trust. We better realize the depth of His love and the abundance of His grace, which enables us to more readily accept the unseen work He does in our lives. We also begin to see that our perspective pales in comparison to His. What we don't know about God would span infinity. But what we do know offers enough perspective to firm up our steps of faith.

A few years ago, my husband and I returned to Yellowstone with our children. We stopped in the same place we had three decades before. The difference astounded and delighted us. Instead of charred earth, stretched a sea of green grass broken up by the purple, yellow, white, and red of various flowers. Lodgepole pines reached for the sky, while strawberries and huckleberries dotted the undergrowth, begging to be eaten.

Sometimes I Forget

Life had sprouted from the ashes. It's a testament to the goodness of a God who controls the universe—a God who transforms the endings we want into the glorious beginnings we need. Trust Him for your new beginning.

> Therefore we do not give up. Even though our outer person is being destroyed, our inner person is being renewed day by day. For our momentary light affliction is producing for us an absolutely incomparable eternal weight of glory. So we do not focus on what is seen, but on what is unseen. For what is seen is temporary, but what is unseen is eternal. (2 Cor. 4:16–18)

Notes

1. *Luther's Works*, Table Talk, 1967 ed. (Fortress Press).
2. Susie Larson, YouVersion, https://www.bible.com/reading-plans/39111-experiencing-gods-presence-by-susie-larson/day/4.
3. Margaret Clarkson, *Grace Grows Best in Winter: Help for Those Who Must Suffer* (Grand Rapids, MI: William B. Eerdmans Publishing Company, 1985), 40–41.
4. Arthur W. Pink, "The Faithfulness of God," The Reformed Reader, https://www.reformedreader.org/aog02.htm.
5. Johann Scheffler [Angelus Silesius], trans. John Wesley, "Majesty and Mercy," public domain.
6. A. W. Tozer, *God's Pursuit of Man* (Camp Hill, PA: Wingspread, 2007), 13.
7. Ann Voskamp, Twitter, November 3, 2016, https://twitter.com/AnnVoskamp/status/794149622725939200.
8. Max Lucado, *The Christmas Candle* (Westbow Press, 2006).
9. John Newton, *The Amazing Works of John Newton*, ed. Harold J. Chadwick (Alachua, FL: Bridge-Logos, 2009), 336.
10. Jerry Bridges, *Trusting God* (Carol Stream, IL: NavPress, 2008), 295.
11. Martin Luther, *Luther's Church Postil*, "Sermon for Third Sunday after Epiphany: Matthew 8:1–13," trans. John Nicholas Lenker, (Minneapolis, MN: Lutherans in All Lands Co., 2022), 450, https://www.lutheranlibrary.org/pdf/504-luther-church-postil-complete.pdf.
12. R. C. Sproul, *The Holiness of God* (Carol Stream, IL: Tyndale House Publishers, 2000), 108.
13. Stephen Charnock, quoted in Arthur W. Pink, *The Attributes of God* (Paris, AR: The Baptist Standard Bearer, Inc., 2013), 53, https://www.standardbearer.org/wp-content/uploads/ebook-files/9781579780210_The%20Attributes%2.
14. Craig D. Lounsbrough, October 26, 2019, Goodreads, https://www.goodreads.com/search?utf8=%E2%9C%93&q=in+my+efforts+to+flee+-God%2C+I+will+always+end+up+some+place+where%27s+He%27s+at&search_type=quotes.
15. A. W. Tozer, *The Pursuit of God* (Harrisburg, PA: Christian Publications, Inc., 1948), 39, https://www.gutenberg.org/files/25141/25141-h/25141-h.htm#Page_33.

16. Deron Spoo, *The Good Book: 40 Chapters That Reveal the Bible's Biggest Ideas* (Colorado Springs, CO: David C. Cook, 2017).

17. Charles Spurgeon, "From Death to Life," sermon, July 26, 1863, Metropolitan Tabernacle, Newington, London, UK, https://ccel.org/ccel/spurgeon/sermons09/sermons09.xxxvii.html.

18. Arthur W. Pink, "The Faithfulness of God," The Reformed Reader, https://www.reformedreader.org/aog02.htm.

19. Philip Ryken and Michael LeFebvre, *Our Triune God: Living in the Love of the Three-in-One* (Wheaton, IL: Crossway, 2011), 20.

20. Anselm of Canterbury, *Anselm of Canterbury: The Major Works*, eds. Brian Davies and G. R. Evans (New York, NY: Oxford University Press, 1998), 98.

21. Philip Yancey, *Where Is God When It Hurts?* (Grand Rapids, MI: Zondervan, 2002).

22. Bob Kelly, *Worth Repeating: More Than 5,000 Classic and Contemporary Quotes* (Kregal Academic & Professional, 2003), 169.

23. David Jeremiah, *Captured by Grace: No One is Beyond the Reach of a Loving God* (Nashville, TN: Thomas Nelson, 2010).

24. Charles Stanley, Twitter (In Touch Ministries @InTouchMin), Apr 28, 2017, https://twitter.com/InTouchMin/status/858080900013338625.

25. Christopher Smart, "A Song to David," http://famouspoetsandpoems.com/poets/christopher_smart/poems/12104.

26. Elisabeth Elliot, "Section Two: God's Curriculum—Waiting" in *Keep a Quiet Heart: 100 Devotional Readings* (Grand Rapids, MI: Revell, 1995).

27. A. W. Pink, "The Impeccability of Christ," *Studies in the Scriptures*, September 1932, https://graceonlinelibrary.org/doctrine-theology/christology/the-impeccability-of-christ-by-arthur-w-pink/.

28. Arthur W. Pink, "The Impeccability of Christ," *Studies in the Scriptures*, September 1932, https://graceonlinelibrary.org/doctrine-theology/Christology/the-impeccability-of-christ-by-arthur-w-pink/.

29. Corrie ten Boom, quote, in an article by Glenn Harrell, https://openhandspublications.com/about/.

30. Andrew Budek-Schmeisser, "Your Dying Spouse 629 - You Only Keep What You Release" *Blessed Are the Pure of Heart* blog post, 6 June 2019, https://blessed-are-the-pure-of-heart.blogspot.com/search?q=I+think+of+Barb%2C+the+dogs%2C+the+house%2C+and+my+very+life+as+mine%2C+and+it+-feels+like+they%E2%80%99re+being+taken+from+me.+But+if+I+willingly+let+go%2C+surrendering+them+all+to+the+God+whose.

31. R. C. Sproul, *John: An Expositional Commentary* (Ligonier Ministries, 2019).

32. G. K. Chesterton, "Introduction," *The Book of Job*, https://www.chesterton.org/introduction-to-job/.

33. "My Life Is but a Weaving," attr. to Florence M. Alt, bef.1892, alt. attr. to Grant C. Tullar, alt. https://library.timelesstruths.org/music/My_Life_Is_but_a_Weaving/.

34. C. S. Lewis, *The Problem of Pain* (New York, NY: The Macmillan Company, 1947), 29, https://archive.org/details/in.ernet.dli.2015.264598/page/n38/mode/1up?q=being.

35. Gustave Flaubert, "Letters to Madomoiselle Leroyer de Chantepie," 18 March 1857.

36. Joni Eareckson Tada quoted in "May 23: Preserve My Life" of Darlene Zschech, *Revealing Jesus: A 365-Day Devotional* (Bloomington, MN: Bethany House Publishers, 2013).

37. Hannah Whitall Smith, *The Christian's Secret of a Happy Life* (Boston, MA: Willard Tract Repository, 1875), 94.

38. Randy Alcorn, *Seeing the Unseen: A 90-Day Devotional to Set Your Mind on Eternity* (New York, NY: Crown Publishing Group, 2017), 167.

39. Elisabeth Elliot, *These Strange Ashes* (Grand Rapids, MI: Revell, 2004).

40. Charles Spurgeon quoted in David Jeremiah, *Stories of Hope from a Bend in the Road* (Nashville, TN: J Countryman Books, 2001), 95.

41. Edward Leigh, *A Treatise of Divinity Consisting of Three Books* (London, UK: E. Griffin, 1646), 879, http://confessionalbibliology.com/wp-content/uploads/2016/05/A-systeme-or-body-of-divinity-consisting-o-Leigh-Edward.pdf.

42. Michael J. Fox, *Lucky Man: A Memoir* (New York, NY: Hachette Books, 2003).

43. Charles Spurgeon, *Spurgeon's Sermons, Volume 06: 1860*, ed. Anthony Uyl (Woodstock, ON, Devoted Publishing, 2017), 41.

44. Albert Einstein quoted in Arthur Austin Douglas, *1955 Quotes of Albert Einstein* (CreateSpace Independent Publishing Platform, 2016), 203.

45. Charles F. Stanley, *Finding Peace: God's Promise of a Life Free from Regret, Anxiety, and Fear* (Nashville, TN: Thomas Nelson Publishers, 2007).

46. Charles H. Spurgeon, *The Treasury of David: Containing an Original Expostion of the Book of Psalms* (I. K. Funk & Company, ed., 1882).

47. Charles H. Spurgeon, sermon, "A Christmas Question," December 25, 1859, https://www.spurgeon.org/resource-library/sermons/a-christmas-question/#flipbook/.

48. Wyatt Graham, "Only the Impossible God Can Help Us Now," March 31, 2020, https://ca.thegospelcoalition.org/columns/detrinitate/only-the-impossible-god-can-help-us-now/.

49. Richard Wurmbrand, *Tortured for Christ* (London, UK: Hodder & Stoughton, 2005), 59, https://www.rwurmbrand.com/pdfs/tfc-english-original.pdf.

50. Wurmbrand, *Tortured for Christ*, 59.

51. Quoted by Connie Rowland on blog post "Healing Scriptures for Comfort and Strength," December 9, 2022, https://mastershandcollection.com/blog/healing-scriptures-for-comfort-and-strength/.

52. Stephen Charnock, "Discourse III: On God's Being a Spirit," *The Existence and Attributes of God*, vol. 1, public domain, https://www.mountainretreatorg.net/theology/The-Existence-and-Attributes-of-God.pdf.

53. William Ames, *The Marrow of Theology* (Grand Rapids, MI: Baker, 1997), 168.

54. Wurmbrand, *Tortured for Christ*, 38.

55. Jonathan Edwards, "Sinners in the Hands of an Angry God," sermon, July 8, 1741, Enfield, CT, quoted in *The World's Great Speeches*, eds. Lewis Copeland, Lawrence W. Lamm, and Stephen J. McKenna (Mineola, NY: Dover Publications, Inc., 1999), 227.

56. William Cowper, (1785) *The Task*: Book VI.—The Winter Walk at Noon line 439 https://www.poeticous.com/william-cowper/the-task-book-vi-the-winter-walk-at-noon.

57. "It Matters To The Master," 2013, song, songwriter Rachel McCutcheon, recorded by The Collingsworth Family. https://www.sghistory.com/index.php?n=I.ItMattersToTheMaster.

58. Frederick Martin Lehman, "The Love of God is Greater Far," 1917, public domain.

59. Charles Spurgeon quoted in L. B. Cowman, ed. Jim Reimann, *NIV Streams in the Desert Devotional Bible: 365 Thirst-Quenching Devotions* (Grand Rapids, MI: Zondervan, 2012), 626.

60. A. W. Tozer, *Experiencing the Presence of God* (Grand Rapids, MI: Bethany, 2010).

61. Frederick Buechner, *The Magnificent Defeat* (1966).

62. Janet Erskine Stuart as quoted in *Suffering Is Never for Nothing* by Elisabeth Elliot (Nashville: B&H Publishing, 2019), 14.

63. A. W. Tozer, *The Pursuit of God* (Harrisburg, PA: Christian Publications, Inc., 1948), 65.

Sometimes I Forget

64. Robert Burns quoted in Earnest Claiborne, *Faith = Success: Go Ahead, Walk on Water* (Dallas, TX: Saint Paul Press, 2011), 164.

65. C. F. W. Walther, "Concerning Predestination," sermon, December 25, 1881, Macoupin County, IL, https://blog.cph.org/study/new/c-f-w-walthers-sermon-on-predestination.

66. C. S. Lewis, *Mere Christianity* (New York, NY: HarperCollins, 2001), 170.

67. Martin Luther quoted in Judy Gordon Morrow, *The Listening Heart: Hearing God in Prayer* (Ventura, CA: Regal, 2013), 199.

68. Stuart K. Hine, "How Great Thou Art," 1949.

69. Hazrat Inayat Kahn quoted in Lynne Twist, *The Soul of Money* (New York, NY: W. W. Norton, 2003), 241–42.